# Media Capital

THE HISTORY OF COMMUNICATION

Robert W. McChesney and John C. Nerone, editors

*A list of books in the series appears at the end of this book.*

# Media Capital

ARCHITECTURE AND
COMMUNICATIONS IN
NEW YORK CITY

*Aurora Wallace*

University of Illinois Press
Urbana, Chicago, and Springfield

© 2012 by the Board of Trustees
of the University of Illinois
All rights reserved
Manufactured in the United States of America
1 2 3 4 5 C P 5 4 3 2 1
∞ This book is printed on acid-free paper.

Library of Congress Cataloging-in-Publication Data
Wallace, Aurora.
Media capital: architecture and communications in New York City /
Aurora Wallace.
p.   cm — (The history of communication)
Includes bibliographical references and index.
ISBN 978-0-252-03734-4 (hardcover : alk. paper) —
ISBN 978-0-252-07882-8 (pbk. : alk. paper) —
ISBN 978-0-252-09452-1 (e-book)
1. Mass media and architecture—New York (State)—New York.
2. Press—Social aspects—New York (State)—New York.
3. Corporate image—New York (State)—New York.
4. New York (N.Y.)—Buildings, structures, etc. I. Title.
NA2543.M37W35      2012
725'.23097471—dc23      2012010495

# Contents

# Acknowledgments

I am enormously grateful to all those who have helped me think through the contents of this book and provided support of various kinds along the way. Faculty and fellow students at McGill University in the Communication and Architecture Departments were invaluable in the earliest stages of this research, most especially Will Straw, whose breadth of knowledge, unrelenting enthusiasm, and collegiality can never be overstated. In New York, Ken Jackson at Columbia University was most generous with his time and his encyclopedic knowledge of New York. At New York University (NYU) my first colleagues, Jonathan Burston, Ted Magder, and Neil Postman, gave invaluable feedback and moral support.

A great debt is owed to the remarkable librarians who have helped at every turn to track down hard-to-find information in their vast collections, most especially those in the Manuscript and Library Division of the New York Public Library, the New-York Historical Society, the Library of Congress, the Tamiment Library of New York University, the Avery Architectural Library at Columbia University, and the Harry Ransom Center at the University of Texas–Austin Library. Along the way several individuals were especially helpful, including Alexa Pearce at the New York University Library, Art Miller at Lake Forest University Library, Robbi Siegel at the Museum of the City of New York, and Thomas Lisanti at the New York Public Library. This work was supported by grants from the Graham Foundation for Advanced Studies in the Fine Arts, the Social Sciences and Humanities Research Council, and the Fulbright Foundation. The European Association of Urban Studies, the Nineteenth Century Studies Association, the American Studies Association, the Journalism Historians Association, and the Society for Cinema and Media Studies have provided collegial space for the consideration of this material, and it is stronger for the comments provided by their members. Daniel Nasset at the University of Illinois Press stewarded this project to its conclusion, and I cannot say enough about his grace and style in doing so. Tad Ringo and Terri Hudoba provided invaluable eleventh-hour assistance.

The preparation of this manuscript was aided in no small part by several researchers, a group of truly gifted current and former graduate students in the NYU Department of Media, Culture, and Communication who have helped make this work better: Melissa Aronczyk, Jessica Shimmin, Cynthia Conti, Magda Sabat, Song Chong, and Kari Hensley, each of whom are a joy to think with. At NYU I am blessed with great friends I am lucky to call colleagues and vice versa. I have no idea how you all do what you do with such grace, but I try to learn from your examples every day. Anna McCarthy, you are the model for how to get everything done with style, enthusiasm, and brilliance. Ben Kafka, thank you for getting yourself and so many talented others hired. Sue Murray, there are no words, but thanks to you, there are words on these pages. Enormous thanks also go to the little ones: Alma, Munro, Pancho, Pippa, and Pip, because you make New York more than a little bit better every day, and to my parents who should visit more.

This book is dedicated to John Paton, who speaks fluent architecture, is a poet farmer, and knows more about newspapers than anyone. And he wrote the poem that inspires this book:

I don't know how
the subway works
Or exactly where
the big building named after the five and dime is
Or why
the university is purple
I don't know why
they call the park central
Or the names
of the five streets with only three letters
Or is it
the names of the three streets with only five letters
I don't know why
time singular is on a circle
Or why
times plural is on a square
Or why
there is no time at all on the triangle below canal
I don't know how
they managed to fit
the whole world in the lobby of a building on 42nd Street
Or how
in Manhattan
You can stand in places that aren't even there anymore
But she does

# Introduction

The current round of handwringing over the future of news journalism is new, perhaps, only in iteration, not in spirit. It continues a long-standing tradition in the media industry that can be traced back to at least the moral wars of the 1840s, the critiques of the scandal sheets of the 1870s, the yellow press debates of the 1890s, the tabloid frenzy of the 1920s, the fears over consolidation, the threat posed by radio, television, and the Internet—and may have more in common with these crises than is normally appreciated. Which is another way of saying that print journalism, and the mass media more generally, have from their inception been in a state of crisis, and to the extent that at a given point in history people come to believe there is a dire threat facing the media as an industry, we learn about this problem via the media. Most often, such crises are worries of the industry itself rather than any grassroots or citizen-led fear over an apparent loss. This perpetual state of crisis in the media industry has also provided justification for actions that might otherwise have seemed unpalatable. Every generation of media has experienced and responded to a threat of some kind that is articulated in terms loftier than a simple loss of profit and has sought techniques for its amelioration. Strategies of consolidation and concentration, cutbacks and cash outlay, competing plans for reform, appeals for regulation and deregulation, tax incentives and breaks, have all been constitutive of how this threat is manifest to the public. Less documented among these strategies, as I argue here, is architecture, which has served in no small capacity to shore up legitimacy in moments of doubt.

In nineteenth-century New York, the Fourth Estate used the tall building to eclipse the old First Estate—the church spires that until then had ruled the skyline of America's most powerful city. Building as much for each other as for the public, newspaper rivalry manifested itself in increasingly tall and bold purpose-built structures, and new additions on top of existing buildings. Publishers chose the most important architects of their day to design large, classical structures with towers, domes, columns, and pilasters based on Italian Renaissance campaniles, French Second Empire chateaus, and Gothic churches. By evoking the classical past of architecture, publishers intended to convey permanence, authority, and stability to their readers, and to lend much needed credibility to their enterprises. Hoping that highbrow, aspirational architecture could be used to elevate and mask their more base and commercial motives, the news business adopted architectural forms from the Old World—architecture to inspire the awe of church design and the authority of the altar, even as it evoked the magnificent castles of Medici princes. The new towers adopted these classical styles, the *New York Times* wrote, "like a self made man going in for culture late in life."[1] The appropriation of these forms helped to situate early publishers as community leaders, public servants, statesmen, aristocrats, and patrons of culture that they hoped to be, all the while establishing a new platform on which media was to be judged.

When the Tribune Tower first overtook the Trinity Church spire on the skyline, it was a gesture intended to show the momentum of progress and the dominance of mass communication as the more authoritative source of information. As if in reaction to Victor Hugo's pronouncement "this will kill that," that the printing press would ultimately overtake the architecture of the church, museums, and monuments as the dominant mode of information dissemination, the *New-York Tribune* employed architecture as its rejoinder. It would challenge the church in both message *and* architecture. Newspapers were, of course, operating within a dramatic era of social transformation of which they were cause and result, and the battle for late-Victorian morality was fought in their pages. Their authority to socialize city people into bewildering new circumstances was maintained by their ambitions toward comprehensive news coverage, and these ambitions were bolstered by equally majestic and self-important architecture. Newspapers sought to enhance their position relative to religion—ideologically by setting new standards of morality and discourse in the paper, and by setting new standards of height superiority on the skyline. Height became a euphemism for supremacy, placing the buildings and their occupants on a higher plane. The repeated entreaties to God, the use of the sun beam or ray of light in their graphics signaled not only visibility but truth, goodness, and righteousness. As Walter Lippman wrote, the press "is like the beam of a searchlight that moves restlessly about, bringing one episode and then another out of darkness into vision,"[2] and in their architecture this beam of light found material form.

The twentieth century brought a new architectural vocabulary of modernism, functionality, and more streamlined forms to newspapers in an attempt to maintain cultural legitimacy in the face of competing sources of information. Using the new promotional tools of advertising and public relations, architecture was incorporated into campaigns that heralded newspapers' continued relevance. Long before the language of branding was commonplace, the conflation between the character of a news organization and the character of its building was made clear through the particular way in which a new building and its construction were reported. In editorials, advertisements, and general reporting, the architectural agenda was set in the press, first to show the public how to interpret and appreciate these new headquarters, then as a way to establish architecture as part of their larger agenda of legitimization. The rise of architectural criticism in the press functioned not only to help the papers advertise their own industry, but also instructed the public to read the city and its structures according to the press's own goals. These printed appreciations stressed their infallibility, their longevity, and their strength, suggesting that readers take the superlatives used to describe the buildings as equally applicable to their news content. Despite the relatively unambiguous message that is communicated in the announcement and construction of a new building, it was not always assumed that there was a universally understood set of symbols or meanings for "great" architecture, or that readers, clients, or passersby would automatically be able to glean what a particular building was all about. Hence, using the tools of the media itself, these companies put their own publicity machines to work on the project of both explaining and celebrating each new building. Often this involved a series of architectural appreciations before, during, and after construction; advertisements in competing papers to inform potential tenants of the availability of space; placements in guidebooks; and the production of other ephemera including stationery and postcards.

Like news, in which nothing can be written until something happens, the construction of a new building provides the occasion for the delivery of content. In the press, as Lippman wrote,

> something definite must occur that has unmistakable form. It may be the act of going into bankruptcy, it may be a fire, a collision, an assault, a riot, an arrest, a denunciation, the introduction of a bill, a speech, a vote, a meeting, the expressed opinion of a well known citizen, an editorial in a newspaper, a sale, a wage-schedule, a price change, the proposal to build a bridge. . . . There must be a manifestation. The course of events must assume a certain definable shape, and until it is in a phase where some aspect is an accomplished fact, news does not separate itself from

the ocean of possible truth. . . . The more points, then, at which any happening can be fixed, objectified, measured, named, the more points there are at which news can occur.[3]

For the press, architecture supplied a "definable shape," a hook on which to hang some news about the media itself. In this way new headquarters are a more permanent version of the "Who We Are" statements made at the beginning of any new venture. They are a position statement, announcing what the company will and will not do, what it would and would not be for. In corporate culture these are known as "mission statements" espousing the values and goals of the entity. They are carefully crafted and resistant to change, but can be amended when a company decides on a new mandate or direction. Unlike statements made on paper or in annual reports, however, architectural statements are expensive, long-term investments requiring close attention to what is being communicated. In corporate narratives, stories of origin and growth are used to embellish the tale of perseverance, the myths of market liberalism and individual mobility, and survival of the fittest. The story of the lone inventor or tinkerer, who through hard work and determination builds an enterprise of substantial size, is commonplace. For the first mass market newspapers, classical architecture provided the appropriate narrative. By designing buildings that looked as though they had always been there, the idea of history, stability, and longevity could be conveyed even in the absence of a past. When two, and often more than two, papers merged, their pasts were recast to make the coming together of formerly feuding entities seem, somehow, inevitable.

The past is created through symbols, stories, and narratives through what Eric Hobsbawm has termed "invented tradition."[4] In moments of transition and crisis nations have invented traditions to confer authority in the absence of a usable past. Invented traditions, thus, "are responses to novel situations which take the form of reference to old situations, or which establish their own past by quasi-obligatory repetition."[5] Citizens are brought aboard the new project through songs, rituals, flags, costumes, and myriad celebrations that codify new practices carrying the reassurance of convention. What all of these invented traditions and narratives have in common is a desire to communicate the values of the institution through some means other than force or direct address. New formations are streamlined into being through the protective gauze of inspiring imagery, a mellifluous tune, or an affective rhythm, as advertisers have long done.[6]

Using architecture as a delivery mechanism for notions of patriotism, nation building, individual aspiration, education, and moral uplift, the media sought to establish its own authority among its readers and citizens more generally. Hence, "public welfare" is a constant refrain that girded many campaigns for improvement of amenities or services. Fusing the interests of the media with the interests of the people at large, or at least hoping to do so, news organizations sponsored programs for improved sanitation, helping the poor, and civic construction projects, among many others. This required a number of strategic sleights of hand of the "help-us-help-you" variety. Building projects were framed as contributions to the greater good, civic pride, and the provision of spaces and amenities for the public, rather than for the corporate providers. Media companies have long entered into this mode of exchange with their publics: in return for your attention to advertising, we will provide you with something of value, be it entertainment or news or light diversion.

Viewed in this way, the architecture of the media can be seen as a domestic strategy of soft power, a chosen instrument in the battle for civic authority and public relations under the guise of public interest (even when the public interest might be, unwittingly and unintentionally, served). Publishers and other media executives have used architecture to monumentalize and build immortality amidst the daily production of ephemera, promising public uplift through projects of private interest. In the nineteenth century, when the public first began to be perceived, as William Taylor wrote, "as a physical presence—a human aggregate—rather than simply opinion dispersed within the population,"[7] spaces for their convening were designed and planned for, often as we will see, by the media.

Roland Marchand has argued that the skyscraper is but one of many strategies that corporate America employed to reassure the public following the unprecedented consolidation of businesses after the turn of the twentieth century. Other tactics included worker welfare programs such as housing and health care, and the personalization of executives through portraiture and recognizable signatures printed on mailings.[8] But the growth of the skyscraper within the media industry deserves special focus, not only because it, along with the financial industry, was responsible for more tall buildings, but because the media was attempting to fuse the architecture and the product into a single message: that of media itself. All architecture communicates, but in the media industry what was being expressed was that these new forms were the dominant lens through which modern life should be understood.

Yet this public presence is not without its own set of anxieties. Corporate self-presentation, a tool now finely honed on multiple platforms and social networking spokes, has undergone innumerable attempts at clarity and covert operations. To express the identity of a business graphically or via architecture necessitates the construction of certain fictions about the solidity and single purpose of an entity even when neither is immediately known. To make a thing apprehendable in the public mind, to marry an idea with a tangible good, a set of values with the goals of a company, has long been the purview of advertising—but corporate identity advertising goes well beyond printed inserts and thirty-second spots. The Rock of Gibraltar, used by the Prudential Insurance Company, conveys strength and solidity for a company whose transactions take the form of financial statements. Indeed it was primarily the banking and insurance industries that gave newspapers chase for the sky. Beyond the shared goals of physical dominance and market supremacy, however, the power of building tall in these two industries was harnessed for very different ends. For those in the money business, a tall, heavily fortified building was intended to signify permanence and stability, a safe place to keep one's life savings.[9] Insurance buildings had to appear profitable but not profligate, since insurance companies were ostensibly spending their clients' money. In the media, the products are more ephemeral and less cherished, and thus newspapers were less beholden to their public for their architectural extravagances, but the skyscraper forms that these industries adopted were remarkably similar. In finance and media the preferred reading of their buildings was one of trustworthiness. Media companies have used architecture to project an image of their company to the public that made a statement about its own power, yes, but the buildings were also vehicles for communicating a preferred set of values. As Tom Shachtman argues, "As the skyscrapers went up, newspapers and magazines began for the first time to refer to the commissioning businesses as 'institutions,' a word previously applied only to non-profit groups or government branches, and one that pleased the sponsors since it encouraged public appropriation."[10] This has been especially true in the media industry.

As Mark McGurl has written, "Self-representation was a way for the corporation to lay visible claim to a privileged, indeed dominating, place on the landscape of American market culture [and] a way to quell the corporation's anxieties about its odd identic status as a legal fiction." The corporation is real only to the extent that the law and public recognize it as such, and "self-representation may be, among other things, a way for the abstract body of business, corporeal but invisible, to convince itself of the 'reality' and sturdiness of its own existence." But corporate self-presentation through visible symbols and structures also gives the public something to focus on; "To be visible is, after all, to be, for example, a glaring target: of public criticism, or federal antitrust legislation, or the actions of organized labor."[11] Visibility was a preeminent goal among media buildings—Joseph Pulitzer was emphatic in his desire that his tower be *seen*—but by the 1960s, Dorothy Schiff warned her staff not to put a large sign indicating that the South Street plant was the home of the *New York Post* for fear that it might encourage some disgruntled reader to drop a bomb on it. For most in the media industry, visibility on the landscape was not nearly so fraught. The buildings they erected were meant as destinations for the public, not faceless corporate structures impenetrable to the outside world. And if the outside world was a place of anxiety, the news building was there to remind citizens that at least the news could be trusted. Pulitzer's *New York World* may have startled readers daily with the precarious conditions of modern life and the city's infrastructure, but it offered its own 309-foot tower as a safe harbor. The media industry as embodied in tall towers is an argument for relevance, an inescapable structure that stands as a testament to the vitality and utility of the endeavor.

Beyond their own buildings, the New York media have authored an explicit account of urban space and city living. As active stewards of their locations, they are significant for their early role in determining the shape and dynamics of the city, supporting those projects they deemed worthy, and admonishing those they did not. They established architecture, real estate, and land values as important elements of the news agenda, from which they also stood to gain.

Park Row was a node in the larger system of communications in the city, a central site in the urban cultural geography of communications. As in other major cities where newspapers were concentrated—with London's Fleet Street establishing the pattern—Park Row newspapers were near the post office and all of the other major printing services in the city. Park Row was convenient to the Western Union Building at Broadway and Dey built in 1870, and the telephone exchanges at 82 Nassau Street. Proximity to the courts, the financial district, and City Hall meant that the main sources of news were close at hand, and Printing House Square, as Park Row was commonly known, provided an endless supply of news from other newspapers. The geography of New York continues to record the activities of the press in its designations of squares. While the name Printing House Square is rarely used anymore, and Globe Square, named in 1911 after the *New York Globe*, located on Dey Street between Greenwich and West Streets no longer exists, the 1811 Commissioner's Plan for New York that superimposed a grid over most of the island created several irregular spaces to be colonized by the media industry. At every point on the map where Broadway intersects with the crossing of a street and an avenue, a circle or square is created with open spaces, irregular plot sizes, and the opportunity to build large, imposing structures. Herald Square at 34th Street and Times Square at 42nd Street still retain the names given them by the newspapers located there. Had William Randolph Hearst gotten his way, Columbus Circle, would have been Hearst Square. Instead, it is now home to the Time Warner Center.

It is not merely that newspapers record or in some way seek to represent the city, but that they make up, in both senses of the phrase, the city and its public. This book argues that the media are not only a set of circulating forms, they are also places. Place is constructed by the media, and its place moves as the media move. The New York landscape gives form to its media. The tall stately New York Times Building circa 1875 was easily the brick-and-mortar version of its seven-columned broadsheets. The rhetorical flourish and graphic embellishment of Pulitzer's World Building was matched by the extravagances on his page. The tabloid's blocky picture and triple-decker headline page is echoed in Raymond Hood's 42nd Street headquarters, a form, like the tabloid that makes the object seem larger than it is.[12]

Although the contemporary media scene is rife with complaint, regret, and nostalgia over what has been lost, tracing the industry through its built form reveals more continuity than change. The media industry in the middle of the nineteenth century in New York was a bustling commercial enterprise, more enmeshed than apart from market forces. It was sensational and serious, pandering and elevating. It earned private wealth while espousing public welfare. For all of their differences in approaches to news reporting and audiences, however, the New York media have responded uniformly to their competition by turning to architecture as their weapon of choice. Although all used the latest materials and implemented modern technology, they found comfort in familiar styles and rarely strayed from the precedents set by their competitors. Few challenged the notion that architecture was a necessary tool of communication.

The decision of when and where to build a new headquarters in the media industry maps onto other important markers of change. New buildings are symbols—if not necessarily signs—of success. They often go up in defiance of financial instability. They go up when other things are going down, and they go up when there is no money to build them. They go up during crises of credibility, they go up in periods of decline, and they go up when they are under threat by new forms of media. The architecture tells a story of power and stability even when the ledger does not. By looking at the media through its architecture, this book demonstrates how the changing dynamics of the industry brought about by competition, consolidation, and concentration are manifested in spatial organization.

Between 2001 and 2007, three important new gleaming skyscrapers were initiated on the New York skyline on behalf of the media industry. AOL-Time Warner, Hearst, and the *New York Times* all invested enormous sums to erect tall towers in Midtown. As someone who has been studying the media industry's architectural statements for many years, even I was a little perplexed at the sudden building boom. In an era of digital transformation, corporate cutbacks, and industrial outsourcing, how could the ever-threatened news industry justify this expense? Despite what I knew about the history of architectural bravado from the nineteenth century, these new developments seemed risky expenditures in the service of corporate branding at a time when the future of both the news business and the skyscraper form after 9/11 was in question. Then one day the efficacy of the plans was made resoundingly clear during a casual hallway conversation about the media with Amy, my next-door neighbor. "Well," she said, "at least we know the *Times* isn't going away anytime soon, they just built a new headquarters on Eighth Avenue." And with that, all of the inherent contradictions I had been trying to reconcile suddenly evaporated. The symbolic promise of a new tall building, it seems, had paid off.

The Time Warner building on Columbus Circle was to be a world headquarters following the announcement of the merger with America Online. Though the merger did not last, the corporate symbolism of the new structure nevertheless attempted to convey the marriage of old and new media on the site once coveted by Hearst. Meanwhile, plans were being drawn for a Hearst Tower at 57th Street and Eighth Avenue, just a few blocks south, the realization of a building that began in the 1920s. The six-story structure that Joseph Urban built for Hearst was imagined as the base of a tall tower to house all of the Hearst operations, but the Depression prevented the work from proceeding. With Norman Foster's forty-six-story tower eighty years later, a quite literal old-media/new-media merger has taken place.

The organization of this book details, in roughly chronological order, how these three buildings came to be, from the development from the early concentration of the news industry in lower Manhattan to its present day manifestations in Midtown to early signs of a return to the area around Park Row. Each era of media building is also explored through the construction of new spaces for public gathering and the forward-looking statements made about the media industry. In chapter 1, the first two papers of the penny press of the 1830s, the *New York Sun* and the *New York Herald*, are examined through their transition from tiny four-sheet bulletins printed out of cramped rookeries to important urban institutions with increasingly immodest architectural ambitions, giving new city inhabitants signposts on the landscape that recalled both a recognizable old world and reassurances of the new. The city and the newspapers shared a common set of values—industrial capitalism, specialization of labor, geographic concentration, and an intricate and specialized economic structure—that materialized in the form that media architecture began to adopt. The parallel development of the city and the newspaper industry shows their forms coming to mirror each other in the segmentation of neighborhoods and news sections.

The *New-York Tribune* and the *New York Times* were the first in the industry to use skyscraper architecture as the medium for corporate image construction, and in chapter 2 they are viewed in the context of the growing power of the press. In the last quarter of the nineteenth century, the city was reimagined with new patterns of circulation, spaces, conduits, and nodes of power. Alongside the growth of the banking and insurance industries, the press colonized lower Manhattan and the value of land rose precipitously. New construction and printing technology required capital investment and new forms of corporate governance. Media architecture transformed from rented space in low buildings to purpose-built signature buildings with lawyers, press agents, and advertising firms as tenants. The shift to taller buildings reveals a preoccupation with both the symbolic and economic value of the skyscraper, as media content became more attentive to the built environment.

In chapter 3, Joseph Pulitzer's spectacular World Building is set against the moves uptown by the *Herald* and the *Times* that would begin the shift away from the nineteenth-century concentration on Park Row. The taller structures signaled a new corporate presence in the city, as wealthy press barons with seemingly unlimited resources increasingly led the news industry. Publishers like Pulitzer built their offices on the uppermost floors from which they could survey the city, their readers, and their competitors.

Chapter 4 investigates the turn toward modernism embodied by the bold Art Deco structure erected by the *Daily News* in 1930, a new form to house the new form of the tabloid. As New York grew to be the largest city in the world in 1925, the emergence of tabloids and radio changed the media landscape once again. Taking their cues from the enhanced corporate image that the Singer, Woolworth, and Chrysler Buildings had brought to their companies, newspapers advertised with yet taller corporate architecture. The *Herald* and the *Tribune*, two formidable rivals in the nineteenth century, were merged and moved to West 41st Street near the *Times*. Hearst started his *New York Daily Mirror* and Bernarr Macfadden started his *New York Evening Graphic* to rival the popular *Daily News*. The buildings looked not to the past but toward the future, as was befitting a new cosmopolitanism. Raymond Hood's Daily News Building was a dynamic design emphasizing modernity, speed, and motion, emblematic of what Simon Michael Bessie described as "jazz journalism,"[13] while set designer Joseph Urban's 1927 Hearst International Building brought a new theatricality to the form. These forward-looking designs branded the media according to the emerging principles of public relations, iconography, and advertising.

Chapter 5 chronicles the post–World War II conditions of newsmaking in New York once Midtown had been established as the new nexus of the media capital. The industry suffered from consolidation, labor strife, and competition from the emerging broadcast media, all of which sent the print media into architectural retreat. Following the war newer modes of communication and suburbanization made the site of news production less important in the minds of readers, and surviving businesses remained in older, ill-suited buildings, overlooked by the public as sites of news consumption except during the many printing and delivery strikes of the era.

In the epilogue, the recent building programs of the *New York Times*, the Hearst Corporation, and Time Warner demonstrate the importance of corporate image-making through architecture that was established in the news business in the 1870s. These buildings stress transparency and an abiding faith in new technology, and invite the audience once again to participate in the spectacle of media production and consumption. These new structures must be viewed against the backdrop of the digital revolution, the journalistic scandals that have befallen newspapers such as the *New York Times* and the defiant approach to building tall following September 11, 2001. Increasingly, these new structures are designed with multimedia entertainment and global branding as their primary goal, addressing consumers and clients with architectural reassurances of the future prospects of their companies in a climate of rapid change. Demographic shifts in readership and the digitization of news have led these large corporations to meet an uncertain future with consolidated real estate holdings in buildings designed to adapt to new media, convergence, and user-created content using a century-old template.

*Media Capital* places media architecture within the context of media history more broadly, seeing in the buildings clear messages about the power of the press, the nature of the reading public, and the commercialization of media. The title refers not only to New York as a media capital, but also to the power of concentrated capital: the press in the context of modern and late capitalism, its manifestation architecturally in the form of the skyscraper, and the mutually reinforcing relationship between New York City and the media industry. Each new communications medium has promoted changes in architecture and the arrangement of urban space, and these changes provide clues to interpreting the media culture in which we live. By scrutinizing the intersection of media and the built environment we can begin to assess the wider implications for the future of media form, urban land use by the industry, and the potential for meaningful public discourse.

Umberto Eco argued that architecture and the mass media had much in common, owing to their shared appeal to the masses.[14] At the most basic level, he saw them both primarily as forms of communication imbued with the ability to persuade by artfully wielding the rules of argument and grammar. They are both implicitly commercial, operating as profitable businesses, and both belong to the realm of everyday life. Eco argued that both also suffer from misinterpretation and the periodic indifference of their publics. That they can exist in the background without demanding much of their audience's concentration is one of Eco's similarities that this book aims to remedy.

# ONE

# News Capital

Published daily at 222 William Street. The object of this paper is
to lay before the public, at a price within the means of every one,
ALL THE NEWS OF THE DAY, and at the same time afford an
advantageous medium for advertising. The sheet will be enlarged
as soon as the increase of advertisements requires it—the price
remaining the same.
—*New York Sun*, September 3, 1833

On its very first day of publication, the *New York Sun* inserted itself into the
landscape of the city by laying bare its location, publisher, and mandate.
The paper's ubiquity on street corners, with its headlines readily visible and
accessible to passersby, moved printed material into the realm of the public

Postcard of Park Row and Bridge Entrance, ca. 1906. (Author's collection)

and out of the rarefied seclusion of taverns, clubs, and domestic spaces. Its one-cent price was the final blow to the stodgy mercantile papers that came in the mail. For a penny even the poorest laborer could indulge at least occasionally, and to lure these new readers the content and the form of the paper changed radically as well.

The partisan and mercantile papers of the seventeenth and eighteenth century contained little that we would consider news by today's or even nineteenth-century standards. They were composed of shipping news that would often be weeks old at the time of printing, and only received by subscribers several weeks after that. The main source of news was correspondence from people at a distance, and its mode of circulation was revealed in the names given to many of these early papers: "Post," "Mail," or "Courier." Once received by the editor-publisher, these news items would be selected, anthologized, and listed, rather than arranged, on a page of newsprint. The jobs of editor, publisher, and typesetter were conflated into one undifferentiated set of tasks in which the main objective was the gathering and display of items from elsewhere. With the emergence of the penny papers, of which the *Sun* was the first in New York, these tasks were separated and specialized. The paper could no longer simply rely on news from elsewhere, and it had to be more current to have a new, consumable product every day. To fill these pages, an entirely new approach to "news" and "information" was taken, to include not only what some segments of the population might need to know to carry out business transactions, but what the larger population could be persuaded to *want* to know. As *Sun* historian Frank O'Brien has shown,

> It was hard to get out a successful daily newspaper without daily news. A weekly would have sufficed for the information that came in, by sailing ship and stage, from Europe and Washington and Boston. Ben Day was the first man to reconcile himself to an almost impossible situation. He did so by the simple method of using what news was nearest at hand—the incidental happenings of New York life. In this way he solved his own problem and the people's, for they found that the local items in the *Sun* were just what they wanted, while the price of the paper suited them well.[1]

This new journalism involved new strategies for news gathering: to seek out the events as they were taking place and to present them in a manner consistent with the narrative storytelling of fiction. Whereas discrete items of news from many different papers had once been placed on a page without regard for context or consistency, items were now written into short narratives with characters, contexts, and structured beginnings, middles, and ends. This embellishment became a hallmark of the "penny press" that would aid drawing readers in, as well as filling page space. The manner of daily publication also ensured a new market of buyers the next day, since no one issue of the paper could possibly tell the whole story of the lived experience of the city.

The centrality of New York as a dominant shipping port providing the gateway from the Atlantic to the inland United States made it a propitious center for newspaper development. The confluence of major waters is a necessity for any major trading city, but the bay where the Hudson River, Long Island Sound, and the Atlantic Ocean come together puts Manhattan Island on "the finest harbor in the Western Hemisphere."[2] These deep, ice-free waters could accommodate hundreds of ships at a time, and being first to receive the news from Europe, New York traders were in the best position to relay information to the rest of the country. Acknowledging this position of privilege, printers who needed to make extra money between contracts began to use their presses to gather and document this information. What Michael Warner noted in his exploration of the press in colonial America was still largely true in the nineteenth century: "Like other capitalized trades of the period, [presses] were almost always in the seaports; and printers had a very special relationship with the merchants and ship captains."[3] The long, protected waterway leading from the ocean into the bay allowed small craft to sail out just as far as the ocean to meet larger ships; small news boats would compete with each other in reaching the large cargo ships before they docked at New York.

The shape of Manhattan Island promoted the development of an incredibly dense, congested, and heterogeneous city, and the natural boundaries of the land mass forced settlement into the southernmost tip of the island nearest to the docks. The easy accessibility to water on three fronts made this property the most desirable for any commercial venture, and the lack of efficient land transportation encouraged concentration in this small area. While some immigrant groups settled together to form small neighborhood communities, these were often overlapping and shared, causing a multicultural intermingling that had been previously unknown in Europe. This concentration of difference existed against the conflicting demands of maintaining cultural and ethnic ties and assimilating to a new urban American way of life. This diversity, somewhat paradoxically, was also an advantageous precondition for the growth of a new uniform mode of communication. The newspaper provided the backdrop to "the seemingly Babel-like confusion of languages, world views and moral codes," that in Rolf Lindner's analysis helped to "break down prejudices and find a way to a common 'universe of discourse.'"[4]

In the dense area of lower Manhattan there was no single unifying religion, and little incentive to create one; religion was never an essentializing characteristic of New York. Unlike the other major cities developing in the United States in the seventeenth and eighteenth centuries, New York was always a mercantile, commercial outpost. It did not suffer the religious Puritanism of Boston or Philadelphia because it was settled as a company rather than by religious fervor or nationalist expansion. Commissioned by the Dutch East India Company, the first settlers at New Amsterdam were traders, instructed to open up a new market for what was then one of the largest corporations in the world, and the company practiced religious and cultural tolerance in an attempt to encourage settlement. These early patterns set an enduring precedent for New York; it was, and still is, one of the most multicultural cities in the world, often dominated socially, culturally, and economically—but never numerically—by one group. By 1890, New York "contained more foreign born residents than any city in the world" and "four out of five people living in greater New York in 1890 had either been born abroad or were of foreign parentage."[5] This unprecedented religious and cultural heterogeneity was a boon to the emerging newspaper industry.

The rise of secularism was both a necessary precursor and a result of the growth of newspapers in the nineteenth century. Although the emergence of the telegraph was largely articulated through the ecclesiastical discourses of electrical transcendence, it was one of the main catalysts of a universalizing, nondenominational, American culture. Foremost among the achievements of the telegraph was the "fostering [of] a national commercial middle class," which was crucial to the growth of the city and the newspaper.[6] Alongside this new commercial middle class was a belief in the power of the press to cultivate a free flow of information that would end religious, social, and racial prejudice and be the main instrument of democracy in America; these discourses of social progress were as common to the popular conceptions and justifications of the modern newspaper as they were to those of cities.

The new technologies of transportation and communication that emerged during the nineteenth century laid the groundwork for urban life in America. The railroad and the telegraph, perhaps two of the most important advances of the modern period, both bound the nation together and created concentrations of people, wealth, commerce, and industry in burgeoning cities. The telegraph allowed information about goods to travel faster than the goods themselves, creating a new market in commodity speculation that allowed for the collapse of space and time for the purposes of trading, yet also encouraged the development of major hubs of concentrated financial power.[7] As a central node in the telegraph network, New York quickly became one of these concentrations, and newspapers followed this flow of resources to report and document it, capitalizing on the need for better, faster information.

The increased rate of exchange between urban and rural areas that resulted from the expansion of the telegraph meant that the social repercussions within cities, in which huge fortunes were amassed and technological and scientific gains had their vanguard, were felt outside cities as well. No longer were small towns characterized by their own particularities in speech or custom; the mobility that the railway ushered in led to a general blurring of distinctions among the previously separate and isolated areas. While this blurring may be understood to have produced a leveling of culture across the nation, cities quickly and irrevocably took their place above rural areas in the sociocultural hierarchy, establishing a primary position in matters of style and taste that the major urban newspapers were central in validating. Despite the fact that the telegraph made it possible for news to be printed at the same time in small towns as it was in the city, New York newspapers managed to maintain their prominence in the industry by establishing a monopoly over news through press associations like the Associated Press, formed in New York four years after the advent of the telegraph in 1848, which kept nonmembers at their mercy for the most important news. And while information was increasingly traveling between the cities and rural areas, intraurban communication was still problematic. Neither the telegraph nor the railroads were efficient means of communication within cities. Free urban mail delivery was not established in New York until 1863, and the telephone not until 1876. The lack of cohesion among city residents that resulted from these limitations in the communication infrastructure provides some insight into the common characterization of cities as anonymous, unfriendly places, but it was a circumstance that the metropolitan newspaper was largely successful in exploiting and overcoming. The newspaper constructed a new urban community, both literally and figuratively, by promoting the formation of those structural components that constitute the very built environment of the city, making urban development integrally bound to that of the newspaper.

Beginning in the 1830s, a new era in newspaper organization, and what many have referred to as a "new journalism," was initiated.[8] These early papers, known as the penny press after Benjamin Day's one-cent experiment with his *Sun*, represented a break from the old-style partisan press that characterized news of an earlier era. One hundred years after John Peter Zenger's landmark libel suit led to the establishment of freedom of the press in the First Amendment, it had become both politically possible and economically desirable to publish "news" that was not entirely in the service of a particular party or mercantile interest. Relying on the sale of advertising space rather than party sponsorship or paid subscriptions for financial support, the penny papers began to concern themselves with an agenda not linked to the interests of a particular group, but of the population at large. These new penny papers were sold on the street corner, rather than by subscription, making their focus more local than international and their information temporally specific.

The biggest story of the nineteenth-century metropolitan newspapers was, as Gunther Barth so succinctly put it, life in the big city itself,[9] and the newspapers arranged themselves physically to take the best advantage of this story. Newspapers in New York were concentrated along the short

Park Row, ca. 1840s.

diagonal street facing City Hall known as Park Row in order to be physically close to all of the central features of the city. From City Hall came all of the political news, and a few blocks away Wall Street was the source of financial news. The ports along the East River made shipping and foreign news easily accessible, and the police, and nearby Five Points slum, provided endless fodder for stories of crime, scandal, and injustice. This area had already been established as the center of printing and publishing activity for its easy access to the ship- and railway-supplied paper. In the pretelegraph era, the *Sun* used horse expresses, trains, and news boats for news gathering to keep a current and steady flow of news coming in. In 1835 it began to use steam power to run its presses, making it possible for a story to go from the streets to the pages within a few hours. The *Sun* capitalized on the city as its muse, and recognized the potential in rallying a new and growing assortment of readers around the daily occurrences of city life. Day's *Sun* sought to break the elitist monopoly on news that had dominated in the previous century by redefining the very concept of news. Although its headlines were small, and the text minute and dense, the early penny papers were indeed more sensational than anything that had come before. Yet for most of its existence, the *Sun* occupied one of the most unassuming headquarters of any business in the city.

Day began his newspaper in the building that was his printing shop, a small rookery that produced a fittingly small paper. The first penny paper scavenged for news from every available source with a skeleton staff, and it was laid out on a sheet of paper eight by eleven inches.[10] Despite its size and lack of resources, the *Sun* was a successful experiment in independent news reporting and dissemination. In its second issue, Day ran a want ad that read, "To the Unemployed—a number of steady men can find employment by vending this paper. A liberal discount is allowed to those who buy to sell again," establishing the practice of newsboy distribution that would characterize nineteenth-century newspaper sales.[11] The *Sun* caught and held the attention of New Yorkers with inventiveness and spirit, demonstrated amply in the famous Moon Hoax of 1835, in which it reported in a series of exclusives that a telescope at the Cape of Good Hope had identified a society of fantastical creatures living on the moon.[12]

By the time Charles A. Dana took charge in 1868, after his unceremonious departure from the *New-York Tribune* and politically opportune wartime post, the *Sun* was one of the most widely read and well-respected newspapers in the country. The paper came with a readership of tradesmen, small merchants, and mechanics, which Dana aimed to keep after his takeover. In his prospectus for the new paper, Dana boldly stated that "in changing its proprietorship, the *Sun* will not in any respect change its principles or general line of conduct. It will continue to be an independent newspaper, wearing the livery of no party, and discussing public questions and the acts of public men on their merits alone. It will be guided, as it has been hitherto, by uncompromising loyalty to the Union, and will resist every attempt to weaken the bonds that unite the American people into one nation."[13]

Such direct entreaties to unification and civics would soon become the work of architecture rather than words, but the style and audacity displayed in the writing and editorial content of the *Sun* were hardly mirrored in the outward appearance of its home, which quickly became a symbol of an obsolete era of newspapers. When Dana took over, he bought the 1811 building at Nassau, Frankfort, and Park Row that was vacated when Tammany Hall moved to its permanent quarters at 14th Street and 3rd Avenue. That the previous tenants had been one of the most corrupt political machines in New York's history was not inconsequential to the building's new tenants. Although Dana was staunchly independent, the election of Grover Cleveland had left him displeased with the Republicans, and he knew that his working-class readers were partial to the Democratic Tammany Hall.[14] His paper had to negotiate among these interest groups carefully. His position was so changeable that neither side could count on him for enduring support, but his invective aroused interest in many. The only consistent feature of Dana's editorials was that they were more likely than not to adopt the least popular position on an issue. The *Sun*'s particular distinction was being opposite, and this dissociation from the rest of the newspaper industry was marked equally well in its architecture.

The five-story walk-up that Dana purchased on Park Row for $220,000 was as centrally located as any newspaper operation could hope to be at the time. The building's physical location functioned the same way that the paper itself did—it provoked competitors to want to be near it, to keep an eye on it, and to imitate it. By its own figures, Dana's presence raised the circulation from 50,000 to 100,000 in just three years and by the early 1880s the two-cent *Sun* was leading all other newspapers with a daily circulation of 140,000.[15] It became, according to many journalists at the time, the most well liked of all the New York newspapers, and Joseph Pulitzer was often quoted calling it "the most piquant, entertaining, and, without exception, the best newspaper in the world," a fact that the *Sun* published in its paper

New York Sun
Building, ca.
1914. (George
Grantham Bain
Collection, Library
of Congress)

in 1871.[16] Immediately after taking over the Tammany Hall building, Dana embarked on a renovation to adapt it to the uses of the newspaper, as well as making cosmetic alterations. The most drastic change was the addition of a mansard roof on the top story, built in the Second Empire style, to replace the simple colonial steep pitched roof. The renovation allowed for more usable floor space in the area that would be the paper's composing room, but it was also a fashionable, modern statement to the public. According to the *Architects' and Builders' Guide*, "By elevation and the addition of a mansard roof, the building has been transformed from the somewhat squatty original into a dignified Romanesque edifice of five stories, for one of which the roof must be counted. As it now stands it has a depth of eight feet on Frankfort Street, a front of eighty-five on Nassau Street and a height of eighty feet. The exterior is rather imposing and unique, two beauties of which have been compassed by the very simple addition of the mansard roof, which is at once the most graceful and useful of all modern inventions for buildings."[17]

For all of its modern innovation, however, the *Sun* Building renovation was effected as a stylistic rather than substantive change. It may have served the paper well to make the gesture to eradicate any lingering ties with Tammany on the outside, but on the inside the structure remained largely the same. The *Sun* continued to publish a newspaper of high quality that was paradoxically—to observers at the time—read by poor and working-class New Yorkers. As Janet Steele has argued, it was because the paper was understood to be popular among tradespeople that "polite society spurned the paper."[18] A prosperous newspaper owner with important ties to government and society, Dana himself embodied this contradiction. He did not belong to the social clubs that other owners like Whitelaw Reid frequented, and these clubs did not subscribe to the *Sun*. Such status contradictions were clearly conveyed in the simple five-story building that the *Sun* occupied on Park Row. It was perhaps Dana's unpretentious style that had kept him content with the Tammany Hall quarters well after the surrounding newspapers had begun to build soaring skyscrapers. While the endurance of the little *Sun* Building amidst the progressively taller towers on Park Row might suggest a curious deviation in the corollary between newspapers and their architecture—that as a paper's size, fortunes, and prestige grew so too did its building—the designs for an unrealized tower to house the *Sun* demonstrate that it was, in fact, the exception that proved the rule.

In rising to the challenge posed by surrounding newspa-

Bruce Price design for a new Sun Building, *New York Sun*, February 8, 1891.

per offices at the end of the nineteenth century, the *Sun* ran a full-page story publicizing the latest design by architect Bruce Price, headlined "If The *Sun* Should Try It!"[19] In the center of the page was an illustration of a thirty-two-story building modeled on the tower of San Marco in Venice. It was unlike any other structure at the time in that it was taller and entirely framed with steel, with the sixteen-story shaft of the building made of plain white marble and void of the usual ornamental bays, piers, columns, or moldings. The entrance way was flanked with heavy granite columns and the top of the structure was capped with a large belvedere, on top of which a lantern sat above a steeply pitched roof. On the top of the structure was a shimmering golden sun on the pointed roof with its rays extending outward in all directions, a design flourish to give form to the paper's motto "It Shines for All," and a feature that would become common in news architecture. The office building was a speculative design which, if built, would have been the first and tallest steel-framed building in the city, making it the direct precursor of other San Marco–inspired campaniles like the Metropolitan Life Building, and the American Surety Building, which Price designed several years later. His design for the thirty-two-story Sun Building earned him a place of distinction in skyscraper history, and although unbuilt, the sketch and its publication provide strong supporting evidence that the *Sun* was not unaffected by the building mania that was going on around it, and that it too harbored fantasies of surpassing its rivals in height. In Theo van Leeuwen's view, "It was very much the predictable materialization of frustrated dreams of absolute hegemony."[20]

## The *Herald*

The *Sun* had a circulation of 20,000 by 1835 when it entered into competition with its most formidable rival, James Gordon Bennett's *New York Herald*. The *Herald* was responding to the seemingly unlimited audience of readers with an insatiable appetite for news that Benjamin Day had discovered, and devised a way of serving them even more successfully than had the *Sun*. Bennett did not have printer's experience like Day, but he did have editorial experience and a formal education. In the May 6, 1835, specimen copy of the *Herald*, Bennett published his prospectus:

> We shall endeavor to record facts on every public and proper subject, stripped of verbiage and coloring, with comments when suitable, just,

independent, fearless and good tempered. If the *Herald* wants the mere expansion which many good journals possess, we shall try to make it up in industry, good taste, brevity, variety, point, piquancy, and cheapness. It is equally intended for the great masses of the community—the merchant, mechanic, working people—the private family as well as the public hotel—the journeyman and his employer—the clerk and his principle. There are in this city at least 150,000 persons who glance over one or more newspapers every day. Only 42,000 daily sheets are issued to supply them. We have plenty of room, therefore, without jostling neighbors, rivals or friends, to pick up at least twenty or thirty thousand for the *Herald*, and leave something behind for others who come after us.[21]

With $500 to start a newspaper, however, Bennett was in a similar position as Day, having to accomplish all of the tasks of newspaper production himself. What he lacked in actual newsgathering resources he, like Day, made up for in inventiveness. The *Herald* pioneered many of the news gathering techniques that would become staples of the newspaper industry. It was the first to take full advantage of railroads, steamships, and the telegraph to get news, and deployed more of its staff to cover these sources than any other paper. The *Herald's* fortunes were so implicated in the success of the telegraph that the paper's methods for receiving the news often became the news story. The *Sun* and the *Herald* employed reporters—a new occupation, if not yet a profession—on the newspaper landscape. The reporter represented a new, proactive approach to news making arising from the penny presses' increasing awareness that the more comprehensively they could cover the city, the more issues they would sell. In stretching the limits of the reportable, the *Herald* dispensed with the sanctity of genteel nineteenth-century modesty; social taboos were broken and the private was made public to a growing population of readers. All classes were given access to the previously guarded secrets of social hierarchy through techniques of scandalizing documentary and exposé and the paper became an essential socializing agent in a city where class distinctions were becoming increasingly blurred.

Although Bennett claimed not to know who his readers were, clearly he was differentiating himself from the working class by publishing the newspaper of respectable society—less base than the other penny papers, and yet more engaging than the financial papers. Despite this position, which was implicitly aimed at besting the popular *Sun*, the *Herald* was nevertheless involved in as much scandal as any of the other penny presses. Bennett is credited with having developed the journalistic techniques of publishing interviews, transcripts, and detailed coverage of crime. He made sport out of ridiculing Victorian sanctity, testing the limits of polite society and enthusiastically flouting them. He taunted readers with the use of language previously forbidden in newspapers in order to describe women's legs and undergarments. After a series of such provocations, the "Moral War" of 1840 resulted, in which "bodies of self-constituted vigilantes went about the city making demands on advertisers to forsake the *Herald*'s columns or suffer in consequence," and according to Don Seitz, "men of standing in church and trade united in the effort to efface the effulgent journal."[22]

Although the language of "yellow journalism" had not yet emerged, any contemporary of Bennett's would have used it to describe the *Herald* if it had. With the exception of the large, boldface headlines, little differentiated the tone and content of the *Herald* from its later rivals the *New York Journal* and the *New York World*. In 1869 Junius Browne wrote that "the *Herald* makes a feature of sensation of some part of its news every morning; and, if there be no important news, creates its appearance by typographical display."[23] One of Bennett's early and popular schemes, that according to journalist Isaac Pray "startle[d] the gaping opposition editors at breakfast, with the thought that their own enterprise had been outstripped by the presumptuous innovator," was to publish fake messages from prominent politicians.[24] The *Herald* positioned itself as superior to the other penny papers by using their own strategies against them and usurping the function of the six-penny mercantile papers by providing relevant financial and maritime news for less money.

Historians have speculated that Benjamin Day's downfall was in providing a newspaper filled with want ads aimed mostly at the laboring classes, an audience that was not resilient enough to withstand economic depressions.[25] Bennett overcame this inherent limitation of the penny press by encouraging advertising from anyone who was willing to pay, and the key to the success of the *Herald* may be said to lie in Bennett's pioneering approach to selling advertising space. To keep his newspaper fresh and interesting, Bennett insisted that his advertisers change the text of their ads every day so that they would complement the timeliness of the news rather than being constant year after year. He did not censor or prohibit ads from any business, allowing all manner of medicine manufacturers, abortionists, and fortune-tellers to buy space. This strategy assured the *Herald* of lively reading material and a dependable source of revenue, but also left it vulnerable to charges that the paper was scandalous and immoral. Bennett was not interested in making a virtue of refusing ads from unseemly sources like many of the other papers, which left his the only newspaper for the less savory businesses to patronize.

Bennett withstood the frequent attacks on his paper to build one of the most successful enterprises in New York by drawing on the principles of three of the most important institutions of the nineteenth century: the museum, the department store, and the city itself. Linking these forms together were Bennett's relationships with showman, impresario, and popular museum curator P. T. Barnum and department store inventor A. T. Stewart. Like Barnum and Stewart, Bennett's approach was encyclopedic in scope and spectacular in display. Like the museum and the department store, the newspaper asserted order over a random, and sometimes distasteful, aggregate of objects and made them meaningful through selection, arrangement, and exhibition. Over the course of its history, the *Herald* used these same nineteenth-century principles of presentation for its headquarters in a series of architectural showpieces.

The first major building that the *Herald* occupied was, like its contemporaries, a small and unadorned rookery, directly across the street from the *Sun*. By 1841, the paper was financially sound enough to allow the purchase of a corner lot at Fulton and Nassau Streets on which to build its plant, extending another fifty feet on Fulton ten years later.[26] Though the building was unremarkable in its exterior design and plan, the *Herald* published a four-part feature extolling its virtues with front-page sketches from August 27 to August 30. The articles focused on the internal arrangement of the paper (the building's design inside and out) and how it facilitated the smooth operation of what was becoming one of the most successful papers in the city. The building was laid out in the then-typical fashion with the presses in the basement, business offices on the first floor, editorial on the second, book printing rooms on the third, job printing on the fourth (where they printed handbills for theaters "except for one or two called the cheap and nasties"), and the composing room on the fifth floor.[27] The order of this internal arrangement was emphasized as a structuring principal for the newspaper, and a clear parallel was drawn between the high level of organization of these rooms and the high-quality newspaper that they produced: "A place is prescribed for every thing; mind to scrutinize, supervise and analyse every thing, and a station for the owners to the utter exclusion of all confusion in carrying on the operations of the department under one sole director, the editor, who imparts a unity of purpose, and a congruity to the whole, not to be otherwise acquired."[28]

The *Herald* sought order through display in both its newspaper layout and its architecture. Bennett was cognizant of these same principles elsewhere in the architectural spectacle that was emerging in lower Manhattan. One year after its own building was lauded in the *Herald*, the new A. T. Stewart dry goods store captured Bennett's imagination. On the opening day of what would become known as the first department store in New York, Bennett devoted many generous columns to describing the building: "We yesterday visited this magnificent establishment, expecting to find its beauty and splendor somewhat exaggerated by popular report, but our ideas of its grandeur fell far short of the reality. Our citizens are by this time well acquainted with the beauty of its plain white marble front, which is not excelled by any building in the city for its imposing appearance or for the chasteness of its design. . . . Its decorations, in general and in detail, are of the most chaste and classical description. There is no gaudy gilding or tinsel show to disgust refined taste, but everything is ornate and elegant."[29]

Most revered in Stewart's new retail store was the gleaming white marble facade, giving the building its early nickname, the "Marble Palace," and Stewart, the "Merchant Prince." According to architectural historian Harry Resseguie, "It was the first commercial building in the United States to have marble exterior walls, and from it sprang a vogue for marble which in the next several decades brought an end to the long, depressing reign of granite, brownstone, brick, and frame."[30] The A. T. Stewart store occupied a full block on lower Broadway between Reade and Chambers, with five stories including the basement. The store was organized to give customers full access to the merchandise for the first time in retail history, with prices displayed on every item, obviating the need for barter. The success of the venture was by no means guaranteed, however; contemporaries thought that a store on the shady east side of Broadway would never attract customers, and Stewart's peers doubted that he could ever sell the abundance of merchandise that he had stocked. With the help of several thousand handbills circulated throughout the city streets, Stewart made a public event out of his opening that commanded enough attention to firmly establish the store's popularity. The notices and publicity in newspapers like the *Herald* were key to his success.

It was more than idle admiration that led Bennett to applaud the new A. T. Stewart store; he appeared to have been personally moved by the building's architectural statement.[31] By the 1860s, the *Herald* was surpassing its expectations in circulation, leading all other morning papers in the city.

When the opportunity arose for him to build new quarters for the *Herald* in 1865, Bennett chose the architect of the Stewart store, John Kellum, and found property on the same unpopular and shady side of Broadway. Bennett wanted an architectural statement that would complement his status, and to accomplish this he chose the signature style of the Merchant Prince: a white marble palace. In an uncharacteristically understated announcement, the *Herald* informed readers of its move to the corner of Broadway and Ann as an information notice: "This is the last day that advertisements for the *Herald* will be received at the old and well known corner of Nassau and Fulton. Tomorrow, Easter Sunday, advertisers will find us at work in the new *Herald* building on Broadway, and will transact their business for Monday morning's issue over the handsome new counters of that establishment. The change will be effected quietly."[32] The notice claimed that the *Herald* staff was simply too busy to have an inaugural opening day ceremony, and appeared not to want to make a public spectacle of the new building in the tradition of other newspaper building openings. Despite these professional pretenses, however, there was little Bennett could do to avoid attention being paid to his new building after its illustrious history as one of the premiere attractions of New York.

||| 

After having searched for suitable new quarters for several years, the plot of land that Bennett chose was the one that had formerly housed P. T. Barnum's famous American Museum. Barnum, the impresario, and Bennett, the publisher, had a good relationship in helping each other's advertising needs. This mutual appreciation was furthered by the respect that Bennett had for the American Museum, an exhibition showpiece of the nineteenth century sharing all of the qualities of opulence and splendor that Bennett admired. Bennett and Barnum also shared a fascination with the bizarre and the spectacular, and the American Museum was the repository of both. Bennett's presses often did jobs for playbills and handbills, as well as printing the usual theater notices in the newspaper. Barnum, a master at promotion, exploited the handbill medium to its fullest in advertising upcoming shows, realizing that city streets saturated with handbills stood a good chance of becoming news items in themselves, thus providing a more efficient and economical means of advertising than merely buying ad space.[33] Bennett, too, learned advertising strategies from Barnum, demonstrated in his philosophy of making news items out of advertisements in his own paper and creating demand for the space by publicizing their popularity. Like Bennett, Barnum was not concerned about the reputations of the people who were the source of his income. According to Matthew Hale Smith, "Mr. Barnum's rule has been to give all who patronize him the worth of their money, without being particular as to the means by which he attracts a crowd to his exhibitions."[34] In a strategy reminiscent of Bennett's earlier telegraphing schemes, "Barnum offered the Atlantic Telegraph Company five thousand dollars for the privilege of sending the first twenty words over to his Museum. The notoriety would be worth more than that sum."[35] (Hearst would employ a similar publicity stunt in the twentieth century, commissioning a dirigible to carry the first issue of his paper from its headquarters).

When the American Museum burned down, Bennett, though dismayed to the see the venerable establishment go, was enthusiastic about the availability of the land on the south corner of Broadway and Ann Streets at the foot of Park Row. Barnum agreed to sell him the lease on the land, and seized the opportunity to have the land appraised at a much higher value than it was actually worth. Bennett agreed to pay the outrageously inflated rate, but upon learning he had been cheated, he demanded his money back from Barnum, who quickly responded that the money had already been spent. To exact some revenge, Bennett decided not to publish any reviews or notices of any event Barnum was sponsoring; in retaliation, Barnum organized the theater community to boycott the *Herald* for advertising. As the theater provided a significant portion of the *Herald*'s orientation and revenue, Bennett was forced to give in to Barnum.[36]

Left with what became known as the most expensive piece of land on earth, Bennett had yet to plan or pay for a building to be put on the lot. With so much publicity surrounding the acquisition of the land, he knew that he had to do something impressive while the public eye was on him. His chosen architect was Kellum, one of New York's most prestigious commercial architects, who in addition to being the architect of the A. T. Stewart store, had become famous for his designs for the Mutual Life Company headquarters, the first permanent home for the New York Stock Exchange, and the New York County courthouse in City Hall Park.[37] His twenty-year fascination with the Stewart department store was Bennett's model for his new building, on the former site of another of his most favorite buildings, the American Museum. With such a prominent location on Broadway, and one that people were accustomed to noticing from its days as Barnum's museum, Bennett had very important design issues to consider. According to Deborah Gardner, it "not only had to reflect Bennett's achievement and his standing in the industry, but also hold its own among such nearby architectural treasures as St. Paul's Chapel, the Astor House hotel, and City Hall."[38]

Like the Sun Building, the new Herald Building was a five-story, mansard-roofed structure, but that was the extent of their resemblance. The Herald had much more in common with the museum and the department store than with rival newspaper buildings. Where the Sun was a square, dark redbrick building, the Herald was a gleaming white arcade with majestic rounded fronts on three sides, built on a triangular piece of land. The Herald was an open, welcoming public structure like its museum and department store predecessors, and shared their commercial orientation, with more than one commentator noting its stylistic affinity to bank architecture.[39] Like the museum and department store, the new Herald Building owed its style to the Italian Renaissance, with French Second Empire detailing, "an appropriate urbane choice for the home of a cosmopolitan publication as well as one which was currently very popular in the city."[40]

If the French design motifs were significant for their popularity in New York at this time, they were even more so to the Herald, which maintained important ties with France through the office of the *Paris Herald*, the pre-

New York Herald Building, John Kellum, 1893. (Picture Collection, The New York Public Library, Astor, Lenox and Tilden Foundations)

cursor to the *International Herald Tribune*. The allusion to French culture was easy shorthand for conveying sophistication and cultivation, and contemporary appreciations of the Herald Building drew direct parallels. *The Architects' and Builders' Guide* suggested that "anyone who has ever visited Paris, and there spent a day, exploring the beauties of the Tower, cannot fail to be at once struck with the resemblance which the centre front of the Herald Building bears to one of the most beautiful of the facades of that gorgeous French structure."[41]

The successful styling of the Herald Building derived from an eclectic combination well suited to the complexion of the newspaper. As would soon become standard in news headquarters, it recalled a noble "old world" eminence to evoke tradition and mask its recency, while simultaneously displaying modern technique and materials to signal its suitability for the future. In this, the Herald Building would like so many others declare itself a metaphor, symbol, and epitome of all that the paper wanted to stand for: "The Herald building is a fit representative, just like the American people themselves, coming from all nations, and the *Herald* newspaper itself the great news medium and instructor for all peoples and for all lands."[42] Aligning the paper at once with the migration narrative of its readers, as well as an organ for edifying uplift, the building illustrated the enormous symbolic impact of architecture in selling the news to its readers.

Though John Kellum's Herald Building was widely and positively reviewed, several changes in the newspaper industry in New York affected the paper and prevented this marble palace from being the enduring architectural showcase that James Gordon Bennett had envisioned. In 1868, the same year that Charles Dana took control of the *Sun*, James Gordon Bennett Jr. took over the *Herald*, after proving to his father with his *New York Evening Telegram* that he could run a newspaper. Bennett Sr., increasingly reclusive in his Washington Heights mansion, died there in June 1872. The staff had little confidence that the younger Bennett could manage the *Herald*, and his reputation as an aristocratic playboy did not bode well for the newspapers' continued supremacy. The younger Bennett took on his duties with less editorial acumen than his father, but with a seemingly unlimited budget for newsgathering. He funded many expeditions to the North Pole and sent the correspondent Henry Morton Stanley into Central Africa to find Dr. David Livingstone, the missionary explorer who had been missing for three years. He used the Atlantic cable as his father had the telegraph, spending extravagant sums of money to receive full coverage of international events.

These innovations reassured the staff that the *Herald*'s future was secure, and though the working atmosphere was less congenial than in the past, the paper's leading position in the circulation contest looked guaranteed.

Bennett Jr. ran the *Herald* so successfully for the following decade that his supremacy over its competitors in the field seemed assured. In 1883, however, when Joseph Pulitzer bought the *New York World*, new and more sensational papers brought about radical changes in the industry. All of the Park Row papers responded to Pulitzer by lowering their cover prices, with the *Herald* moving from three cents to two cents. This maneuver cost the *Herald* needed circulation revenue and only served to strengthen the *World*'s position. The competition was waged on the advertising pages as well, and the *Herald* was caught unprepared for the new developments in typographical display. Having pioneered the ad pages in New York, the *Herald*'s dominance in this field had long been established, but when department stores began requesting larger, multicolumn ads to reproduce images of fur coats, typewriters, and other consumer goods, the *World* was more accommodating than the *Herald*. To make up for lost business, the *Herald* increased its advertising rates, which did more damage to them than to their competitors at the *World*. Once the yellow press barons began to compete, the *Herald* found itself in a state of perpetual readjustment. Additionally, the younger Bennett was uncomfortable about the tenants who remained in the Broadway and Ann building under contracts made with his father. The role of landlord was not one that appealed to him, and he began to think about a new home for his paper.

The *Sun*'s commission of an ultimately unbuilt thirty-two-story skyscraper, and the *Herald*'s move uptown to 34th Street, were different responses to the same set of circumstances. The industry that they had built in the 1830s was no longer recognizable by the 1870s by either journalistic or architectural standards. In the middle of the nineteenth century, dozens of newspapers started in New York with the hope of becoming the next big enterprise. Barriers to entry were still relatively low, and print jobbers could make use of dormant presses in off hours to put together random bits of news. New arrivals from elsewhere in the country and abroad provided a plentiful labor force willing to do grueling work, and the close concentration of businesses in lower Manhattan was fertile ground for entrepreneurs. Most papers did not last more than a few years before failing to find an audience or being taken over by a rival—but the number of separate titles in operation at any given time was staggering. By the last quarter of the nineteenth century, the newspaper industry in New York came to be dominated by ever wealthier publishers with access to ever larger amounts of capital, but the dynamics that were put in place remained: the newspaper and the city had become parallel forms, each constructing the other with mutually reinforcing values of industrial capitalism, specialization of labor, geographic concentration, and an intricately complex economic structure. Real estate began to play an ever more important role in the newspaper enterprise, and single owner operations grew into companies with boards of directors who realized the profits to be gained by building larger structures than needed for their own operations in order to rent out floors to income-producing tenants. The increasingly corporatized news industry took form in the architecture each organization adopted, and the public relations value of building large, majestic, showpiece headquarters became an even more central concern.

## Addressing New Publics

The *Herald* and the *Sun* were both successful in identifying and helping to construct a new readership for their growing enterprises. But the traditional narrative that the penny presses were instrumental in the construction of "the mass," is an assertion that deserves at least some consideration. In the mid-nineteenth century, derogatory remarks about the menace of large groups of people were often found in memoirs and writings of the elite, who begrudged the blurring of social hierarchies in the city and the perceived loss of social power.[43] Such sentiments were given academic credibility by social scientists like Gustave Le Bon, who identified the "crowd mentality" as one that was suggestible, gullible, unintelligent, and prone to violence.[44] In midcentury New York, there was certainly evidence available to support such theories, as the city witnessed numerous race, labor, and ethnic riots.[45] For some nineteenth-century commentators, the press was a mechanism for the development of a new democracy in America, providing people with nonpartisan tools for learning more about the new society in which they found themselves. For others, it was merely an agent of distraction that kept people from the more important demands of nation building, the economy, and self-determination. One such observer, writing in the *Democratic Review* in 1837, contended that

> in the city men move in masses. They catch the current opinion of the hour from their class, and from those public organs of the press on

which they are accustomed to depend for their daily supply of superficial thought—for their morning dose of mental stimulus, in those flaming appeals to their passions, their interests or their vanity, which it is the vocation of the latter to administer . . . they are like the men in a troubled crowd, swept hither and thither by the current of the huge mass, with a force which the individual can rarely nerve himself to stem. Individuality in fact loses itself, almost of necessity, in the constant pressure of surrounding example, of the general habit and tone of society, and in the contagious excitements which rapidly chase each other in their successive sway over the multitudinous aggregate of minds.[46]

Most of the voices that came out against the popular press did so in an attempt to maintain the class divisions that worked in their favor, and to guard against intrusion by the working classes. But if Louis Wirth was correct that "the greater the number of individuals participating in a process of interaction, the greater is the potential differentiation among them,"[47] then the theories of the mass are likely mistaken in their claims of homogeneity. While the penny presses depended for their large circulation on a large number of people living in close proximity, the uniformity of this population cannot be assumed. The argument that newspapers led to a debasement of taste and intellect was largely insupportable, given the high quality of writing that was to be found in the major papers; charges of homogeneity and lowest-common-denominator content were equally so in light of the number of successful papers in English, German, Italian, and Hebrew that existed at this time. The "mass media" therefore, may be more usefully reconceptualized in accordance with Marshall McLuhan's argument that they are "mass" only to the extent that many people were engaged with them at the same time.[48] Despite this, however, the popular image of the press as a base, crass, commercial enterprise was prevalent, and needed to some degree to be countered if those in charge of it were to prevail. Architecture was mobilized to smooth over these rifts, to lift the press out of the gutter that critics saw it in, and to align the news not with the mass but with its moral uplift.

The metropolitan newspaper could not exist without a large population living in close proximity, given the street-corner method of distribution, and the state of the urban population was often seen as a result of the newspapers themselves. In its two-dimensionality and preoccupation with surfaces, the paper shared significant characteristics with city inhabitants. Each day, the paper told stories and offered guidance to city people, and this guidance was overwhelmingly superficial and nearsighted. Quick, accessible, and easy-to-follow parables were provided to readers in the form of how-to articles, advice columns, and human interest stories of success in the face of overwhelming odds. This "mass communication" was well suited to a population that Wirth characterized as "impersonal, superficial, transitory and segmental."[49] Their social relationships, according to Robert Park, were like those of people living in a hotel, where people living in very close proximity know very little about each other. "Under these circumstances," wrote Park, "the individual's status is determined to a considerable degree by conventional signs—by fashion and 'front'—and the art of life is largely reduced to skating on thin surfaces and a scrupulous study of style and manners."[50] The newspaper was in both form and function acting as a mirror not to the population generally, but to the kinds of relationships that were being cultivated by the large, impersonal city.

The newspaper also shared a structural similarity with the city, which the newspaper seemed to foster through a series of innovations in layout and design. As papers grew from four- and eight-page sheets with improved printing press technology, the organization of news became more segmented into sections directed at different readers, keeping pace with changing demographics. Sections that divided the news into areas of interest such as sports, finance, crime, and women's news were also beneficial for advertisers' need to place their notices next to the news that would attract their most desired audience. But this early sectioning of the newspaper reflected more than an increasingly specialized and sophisticated view of readers; it was a reflection of the very structure of the city itself. The sections were to urban districts as columns were to streets; the city and the newspaper were at once both compartmentalized and comingling, with discursive space and real space conflated and mirroring each other. As the city grew, the newspaper expanded its scope to cover all of those areas that city dwellers could no longer know personally. This meant intensifying the focus further into neighborhoods, and dividing the city up into beats that individual reporters would be responsible for. The pages of the newspaper thus became an index to the physical space of the city, with street names corresponding to a different social or cultural arena: "Being assigned to 'Broadway,' 'Wall Street,' or 'the Bowery' does not of course mean only being responsible for the theatre, the financial world or social welfare issues, rather that the assignment is based also on a quasi-ecological idea of the functional differentiation of the urban space."[51] This functional differentiation of urban space was represented in the sectioning of newspaper stories, and could be seen, too, in the segmented ethnic and commercial enclaves like Germantown, Chinatown, and Printing House Square.

This ordered disorder manifested itself in municipal planning efforts like the grid plan for city streets and in the newspaper as orchestrated news events and rows and columns of newsprint. The Commissioner's Plan of 1811 that established the grid system north of Houston Street sought to "unite regularity and order with public convenience and benefit."[52] The acceptance of this plan for New York was largely based on a commitment to a "simple and mechanical way" to encourage development, and the "practical concerns of a city plainly commercial in character."[53] As Edward Spann has shown, the acceptance by citizens of the grid formation was "motivated by their indifference (and, possibly, hostility as the citizens of a proud new nation) to practices associated with the European and colonial past."[54] The form and layout of the newspaper in the New World of New York City can equally be seen as aspiring toward a commercial and democratic future, unfettered by the social hierarchies of the past. Newspapers were a central agent in the transformation of the new city, but as we shall see, the classical references in the design of their buildings display some ambivalence about how modernity was best expressed.

# TWO

# New Buildings and New Spaces

And now that we are about to erect on the old site the largest
and most imposing newspaper office in the world, the controlling
thought of the proprietors of THE TRIBUNE is, that here is his
true monument.
—*New-York Tribune,* "The Old and New Tribune Buildings,"
  May 17, 1873

The *New-York Tribune*'s entrance into the newspaper field in 1841 was auspicious not only for the emergence of the boisterous Horace Greeley onto the scene, but also for the tower that was erected in his honor in 1875, although Greeley himself was not around to see it. Greeley and his *Tribune* were in many ways antithetical to the popular newspaper principles established by the penny papers the *Sun* and the *Herald*. The *Tribune*, established in 1841

Postcard of City Hall and Newspaper Row, ca. 1907. (Author's collection)

after Greeley had enjoyed significant success with his publications *Log Cabin* and *New Yorker*, attempted neither the political independence nor the urbanity of its two biggest rivals. Greeley himself was an exponent of the rural life with an interest in agricultural engineering who favored cooperative living and other socialist experiments like Fourierism that were popular in the nineteenth century. He was a vegetarian, a pacifist, and an abolitionist, and his preference for rural life was articulated in his feelings toward urban unemployment, which he supported as a mechanism for promoting westward expansion. In his often-quoted statement, "Go west, young man."

Owing to this predilection for the country, Greeley's *Tribune* was not as interested in crime or other urban issues as the *Sun* or in the machinations of society galas as the *Herald*. Its first issue carried news of President William Henry Harrison's funeral arrangements and public processions, and made Harrison's dying words the paper's motto, printed each day below the flag: "I desire you to understand the true principles of the Government. I wish them carried out—I ask nothing more."[1] Greeley's editorials were aimed at larger national issues like trade unionism and antislavery. It was a vociferously republican one-cent paper in a largely democratic newspaper milieu, when the only other Whig papers were charging six cents a copy. Filling this niche, the *Tribune* established itself as a solid and reliable voice of the party, whose editorial leanings were indistinguishable from those of Greeley's. The paper's second edition implored readers, "We want a good Whig friend to stand at each poll in the City tomorrow, and ask the Whigs, after voting, to take the *Tribune*. Who will act for us! To someone in each District who knows it well, we shall be glad to pay a fair compensation. Call on us to-day."[2]

The *Tribune* became a long-standing, upright paper that was often referred to as the "Great Moral Organ." It was Greeley's initial position at *Log Cabin* that the paper not be used as a gossip sheet or a muckraking tool, and it was in this paper that he outlined the prospectus for the *Tribune* on April 3, 1841, one week before the first issue's appearance: "The immoral and degrading police reports, advertisements, and other matter which have been allowed to disgrace the columns of our leading penny papers, will be carefully excluded from this, and no exertion will be spared to render it worthy of the hearty approval of the virtuous and refined, and a welcome visitant at the family fireside."[3] This commitment to a dignified and distinguished approach to news guided many of the smaller decisions at the newspaper as well. Unlike many of his contemporaries, Greeley governed the paper with authority and kindness toward his workers. He hired skilled writers to work under him, and his editorial perspective was well known and largely supported by the staff. He was unusual in that he did not keep the workers under the constant threat of unemployment as was the custom on Park Row, and as a result, biographers note a strong feeling of loyalty and trust at the *Tribune* during Greeley's tenure. He established the Tribune Association, based on François Marie Charles Fourier's principles, which created a board and profit-sharing structure that was unique in the newspaper industry at the time.[4] Because it was also a well-written and respected paper, ambitious writers from other newspapers aspired to work there, including many of the most famous names in newspaper history, among them, Henry J. Raymond (later of the *New York Times*), and Charles A. Dana (of the *New York Sun*).

While in its early days the daily *Tribune* was not a serious rival to the other papers in New York, the weekly *Tribune* was extremely popular in the rest of the country; and the reconstruction of the nation after the Civil War was one of Greeley's primary concerns. His national profile and his position on the South were largely what led the Liberal Republican Party, with support of the Democrats, to nominate him to run for president in 1872 against Ulysses S. Grant, even though Greeley had been a career Republican and had helped support the Republican Party in the *Tribune*. Though the campaign was unsuccessful, it did not end up having the devastating effect on the *Tribune* that critics thought it would. Nor, as feared, did Greeley's death immediately following Grant's victory.

While Greeley was away campaigning the newsroom was run by Dana's replacement, Whitelaw Reid, with Greeley's trademark conservative independence. Reid never went against Greeley's wishes and continued to avoid personal attacks on political opponents, which made Greeley's run for president all the more grueling, since he refused to respond to the political charges in other papers in an attempt to raise the level of civic discourse. Allowing misunderstandings and contradictions to stand uncorrected, Greeley's advantageous status as a newspaper owner was hardly used to the benefit of the campaign. The difficult and unsuccessful campaign was capped with the death of Greeley's wife in 1872, and Greeley returned to the paper weakened, demoralized, and defeated. Shortly after, in November 1872, Greeley himself died, leaving the *Tribune* without its most outspoken and popular voice.

All concerned were worried that without Greeley there would be little to recommend the *Tribune* as a successful newspaper. This anxiety was felt equally well among the shareholders, who saw the value of their assets plummet. Dana had sold his stock to a patent-medicine entrepreneur, and more and more the *Tribune* was being controlled by accountants and outside interests on the board than by newspapermen. They cared little for the sentimental personal journalism of Greeley's era, and sought to run the newspaper as a profit-making business above all else. The board's view was that the paper had to "be modernized, made smoothly efficient, and protected as a safe investment."[5] They did, however, insure Greeley's life for a sizeable sum, and this return provided Whitelaw Reid with some of the capital he needed to reconstruct the floundering paper. To buy a controlling interest, however, Reid had to borrow $500,000 from one of the least respected businessmen of nineteenth-century America, the financier Jay Gould. This alliance was both unimaginable and antithetical to the program and philosophy of the *Tribune*, but it was a necessary evil in Reid's mind to gain control of the paper. As journalist Selah Clarke wrote, "If you wanted to hurt your esteemed contemporary's feelings in those days—as you did—you said Jay Gould had lent him money."[6]

Not a month after Greeley's death it was decided that architecture should be the chosen instrument to fill the void left by his absence in the public realm. In November 1872, *Tribune* reporter and shareholder Bayard Taylor suggested to Reid that Greeley's life insurance should be used for a new building, to "assure the public of the power and stability of the paper."[7] The work of making a significant statement on the skyline fell to editor Whitelaw Reid, who understood that a symbolic gesture of this kind was necessary to reassure shareholders and readers that the *Tribune* was permanent, solid, and committed after Greeley. Choosing a plot on Park Row then known as the Lawrence block, Reid wrote that "if we get that we shall have a front of over 80 feet on Nassau St. and will then make a building which will surpass any newspaper building in the country, although we are aiming at a showy building."[8] Reid's letters provide evidence that many of the major design decisions predated the competition and selection of the architect, Richard Morris Hunt: "My present inclination is to brick as the exclusive material, not even stone window caps, using three kinds of brick, pressed Philadelphia red brick, the same colored black by dipping in boiling tar or petroleum and a Milwaukee yellow brick of fire brick, with brick moldings for window caps and cornices. I believe you have such buildings in Florence, and I think the Henri IV style in Paris is not unlike it. This will be comparatively cheap. We will make it fireproof, 9 stories high and get a rental of $80,000 to $120,000 through what we can let of it."[9]

Having been an avid traveler and subsequent foreign minister to France (1889–92), Reid would easily have been familiar with the styles to which he refers in this letter. The nine-story height ensured that the tower would be taller than any existing New York office building, and was thus neither an arbitrary choice of height nor one based on the functional space requirements of the newspaper. The design and size of the Tribune building was primarily governed by the enhanced public image that would be garnered for the newspaper, but the added income from tenants was a welcome benefit.

These design guidelines were made more specific in a memo by Reid reiterating that the building must be fireproof, "not less than eight stories tall," that the stories be of suitable height for bankers and lawyers' purposes, and that there be an internal separation made between rented offices and *Tribune* offices, to be facilitated with separate entrances, elevators, and stairs. Reid also demanded "a high tower . . . with an illuminated clock," "at least two if not three ornamental porticoes for entrances," and finally, "provisions to be made somewhere for a sitting statue or other suitable memorial of Mr. Greeley, to be not higher than the second story."[10] This memo was sent to several prominent New York architects, including J. C. Cady and Richard Morris Hunt. The competition for the Tribune building did not follow protocol with an open call and a choice made from official submissions. Reid obviously had a very clear idea of what he wanted the building to look like, and was well aware of who the leading architects of his day were. He made several initial inquiries to well-known architects and also asked for advice from other respected professionals like Frederick Law Olmsted.[11] Reid also made it clear, however, that he would choose the architect based on the merits of the design alone, and not on the architect's name or reputation.

Several designs were submitted, and from them, Hunt's and Cady's remain. Cady's design was a very similar block-and-tower structure with a tower on the corner of the building, fulfilling the design requirements, but several factors favored Hunt. One was that he was known socially to Reid and had received positive recommendations from people like Olmsted, but Reid would also have endorsed Hunt for his Beaux Arts training in Paris, given that Reid was predisposed to the French style of architecture. Hunt had led the team of architects who designed and implemented the United States Post Office at Broadway and Park Row (1868–75) in the immediate vicinity of the Tribune site, and he had also submitted impressive, though ultimately unsuccessful, plans for the competitions of the Western Union Building, the New York Stock Exchange, and the Equitable Life Assurance

J. C. Cady's unsuccess-
ful design for the Tribune
Building. (New-York
Historical Society)

Building. Whitelaw Reid's personal letters reveal a growing obsession with
the building, as his official biographer Royal Cortissoz has noted, "in his
correspondence for the two years of construction the new building crops up
nearly as often as the wickedness of Grantism."[12] Reid wanted his building
to be a part of his larger project of improving the New York aesthetic of the
1870s, and he used the newspaper to educate readers on the merits of his and
other buildings in the city. In 1870 he wrote to the *Tribune*'s architecture
critic Clarence Cook that he wanted "a crisp editorial on the prevailing lack
of architectural taste in New York."[13] The editorial was followed by a series
of articles espousing Reid's own architectural tastes and judgments.

On the basis of Reid's clearly defined vision and Hunt's reputation and
expertise, a tall, new clock-towered structure was designed for the irregularly
shaped lot at 154 Nassau, at the intersection of Park Row and Nassau and

Spruce Streets. As per Reid's directions, the building was a massive, fireproof stone-and-brick structure. Light-colored granite and redbrick contrasted in a striking pattern that helped it stand out against its neighbors, but the *Tribune*'s own appreciation of the building disputed that there was anything superfluous or ornamental in the design: "Every ornament has its uses; the position of every stone is dictated by the necessities of construction; and the whole work exhibits the overruling influence of a consistent idea. It presents, therefore, what comparatively few American buildings do show, a strict architectural design."[14]

The building was intended to attract attention, and though many critics found the brightly contrasting façade comical, the public areas of the building suggested that no expense was spared in pleasing the regular citizens of New York who might visit. The first floor housed the business offices of the newspaper where people would come in to buy subscriptions and place classified ads, and this functioned, in conjunction with the façade, to give the public an impression of the paper as a successful, erudite, and refined organization. Below this floor were the heavy presses of the paper, never on view to the public. The midsection of the building was made up of offices rented out to small businesses—ads in the paper touted these floors as "The Best Lawyers Offices in the City"—and the eighth and ninth floors housed the editorial and composing rooms. The paper took advantage of these upper floors to have the best access to light and air for laying out pages,[15] in addition to the commanding views and the feeling of invincibility that came from having the highest offices in the city "overlooking New York bay and harbor, the North river, and a good part of New Jersey."[16] Inside the tower room at the top, naturally, was the office of Whitelaw Reid.

The height of the structure was of paramount importance to Reid, who from the beginning had requested a nine-story building. During the construction process, however, when it appeared that the nearby Western Union Building might overtake it, the *Tribune* suddenly added another story to make its final height 260 feet to Western Union's 230 feet. The effect of the *Tribune*'s height, however, would have far less effect or influence on Western Union than it would in coming years on the rest of the newspaper industry. The *Tribune*'s closest neighbor, the *New York Sun*, was immediately and drastically diminished relative to the new tower, the fact of which Reid was well aware when he wrote to Bayard Taylor that they had secured the entire property around the *Sun*, and that as a result, the *Sun*'s "nose [was] not a little out of joint."[17]

New-York Tribune,
April 10, 1875.

The distinctive block-and-tower design combined two symbolic elements of nineteenth-century building: a low, massive structure to convey
open, civic, and public virtues, and a tall, thin spire to convey commercial or
mercantile achievement.[18] Such allusions were furthered in the 10,000-word
feature titled "The *Tribune*'s New Home," published in the *Tribune* on the
building's opening day, April 10, 1875. The feature text wrapped around a
large artist's rendering of the new Tribune tower in the center of the page,
romantically narrating the story of the paper and its various homes. Making
clear links between the work of the newspaper and the type of architecture
that housed it, the story told of the transformation from a noble, modest
newspaper in a noble, modest building into an impressive newspaper in an
impressive building. "Though decent enough in that day of small things,"
the old quarters "sufficed" but surely would not be adequate for the impressive *Tribune* of the 1850s and 1860s. From the Ann Street building the

*Tribune* had moved to a larger one in 1842 on the site where the tower would eventually be built. The old building, though small and unprepossessing, was recuperated and redeemed in the nostalgia for the solid integrity of the man who built the newspaper into what it had become. Its story of origin detailed the development from humble beginnings that nevertheless link it to the advancement of a proud nation: "Its stairs were worn with the feet of men whom the future historian of this country will place among the venerable figures in the most critical period of the development of the American Republic; and it was inseparably associated with the progress of American scholarship and culture and enterprise. Long before his death, Horace Greeley saw the realization of his chief ambition assured, and knew that the unpretending brick building on Printing House Square was certain to be a conspicuous figure in the records of his native land."[19]

III

In planning for the new building Reid and the rest of the *Tribune* board wished to maintain the *Tribune*'s physical presence in the city though notable and eye-catching architecture. The process of acquiring land was a lengthy and complicated one, and it reveals an important element in the plans of the newspaper that would influence the final design of the structure. Over a period of several years, the paper saved money and put it into a building fund; as properties became available, it purchased them in sequence until the total lot size was large enough. By annexing several smaller properties the *Tribune* lot was able to have frontage on three different streets, at the intersection of Spruce, Frankfort, and Park Row. A hasty decision to build a new headquarters could never have secured enough land on which to build such an imposing structure. The slow acquisition of lots reveals a purposeful, determined plan that took place over several years, to have the largest and most impressive newspaper building in the city.

For architect Hunt, this aspiration demanded a new kind of structure that would mark the beginning of a new American style. It was not possible to merely adapt common bank- or insurance-building structure to the newspaper office, because the design demands of the editor had been so specific. As critic Barr Ferree wrote, "In the *Tribune* Building Hunt had a problem not before presented to an American architect. It was an office building of a height then deemed appalling, and was a complicated and venturesome enterprise from which many a less cautious man might have shrunk. But Hunt was eminently conservative. His design shows, it is true, evidence of his French training, but it certainly exhibits a marvelous self-control which relatively few of his successors in the designing of high buildings exhibited since."[20]

The new building confirmed to the public that new ownership would not hinder the paper's future stability. Glowing accolades reprinted from other papers in the *Tribune* congratulated the achievement. "So far from the *Tribune* falling into decadence," wrote the *Washington Capitol*, "it never has been so prosperous and so popular." The *Brooklyn Eagle* wrote that "the new quarters into which the paper has moved are fit for princes. We are glad they are to be occupied by princes of the pen." The *New York Evening Post* concluded that "the new building which is to be associated with its name is so prominent an object that it needs little description." In the praise from the Springfield (Massachusetts) *Republican* it seemed that the public relations goals of the new building had been achieved: "The New York Tribune celebrates its 35th anniversary to-day, by taking possession of its new building, which is by far the most ambitious ever erected by an American newspaper. That it should be somewhat lifted up by its well-deserved prosperity is natural. Why shouldn't it be? Certainly the Tribune never was so good a newspaper as it is to-day, never gave better promise for the future, and never came nearer justifying its claim to be the 'leading American newspaper.'"[21]

By the end of the 1870s, under the direction of Whitelaw Reid, the *Tribune* had become an urbane and cosmopolitan daily known for one of the most important monuments of newspaperdom and architecture in American history. As Richard Kluger wrote in his epic history of the *New York Herald Tribune*, "What better way to demonstrate its permanence and allay rumors of its shaky condition than to put up the biggest building in New York?"[22]

## The *Times*'s Great Grey Giant

In the newspaper industry, there were many successors to the *Tribune* as competitors sought to outdo it both on the page and on the skyline. The next to fall prey to the allure of the skyscraper was the *New-York Daily Times*, a paper that in every other way resisted the temptation of ostentation. Henry Jarvis Raymond, who had worked as a *Tribune* reporter under Greeley, introduced the new daily in 1851, as an alternative to the brand of news found in the *Sun, Herald,* and *Tribune.* Its modest entrance into the field was announced in the first issue: "The *New-York Daily Times* published every morning (Sunday excepted) at the office, Number 113 Nassau Street, between Beekman and Ann, just behind the Old Park Theatre, and delivered to subscribers in this city, Brooklyn, Williamsburg and Jersey City for six cents a week."[23]

For the first year, Raymond operated his newspaper out of these small, temporary surroundings while he made preparations for a move, "for they had entered upon the publication of the *Times* not as an ephemeral enterprise, but as a permanent business, and an establishment of its own was regarded from the outset as a matter of the first necessity."[24] In a now familiar story of origin, the paper sought to align the cramped space of its offices with the cramped space on the page. By establishing that there was more demand for content than its form could allow, a move to a larger building was presented as a necessity and a public service: "Owing to the limited size of the sheet, we could neither give as much reading matter daily as we desired, nor afford to take advertisements at so low a price as other papers. We shall endeavor, during the coming year, to obviate these difficulties, so far as possible."[25]

There was integrity to be claimed by refusing many potential advertisers, just as there was some integrity in maintaining such small quarters. It allowed the *Times* to appear less corporate and more trustworthy in an industry where rivals were spending lavishly on elaborate newspaper pyrotechnics. Nevertheless, the *Times* bought two lots that had previously been occupied by the Old Brick Presbyterian Church and graveyard, an impressive site because it was effectively a three-sided corner at the intersection of Spruce, Nassau, and Park Row. The block was not completely flush with the street, creating a large open area in front of the building that made the building's approach much more striking, increased its visibility, and allowed the whole site to eventually become known as the "Times Block." According to the *Times*, the site was "in one of the most conspicuous and commanding positions in the City, and with the exception of the triangle at the lower point of the Park, there is no other location in New York which combines so many business advantages or is so accessible to the great mass of the business community."[26] Another benefit of the site was that the vaults below the ground extended well beneath the road in front, making the available underground space for the presses even larger than the ground level footprint. Many different architects prepared designs for this unique lot, and the one by Thomas R. Jackson was finally selected.

Despite it being a year of general economic panic and building recession, the construction of the new Times Building began in May 1857. Elmer Davis notes that to pay for the building, "a sixty percent assessment was levied on stock, and all profits above twenty percent a year were set aside for the time being for a building fund. The *Times* was making money—enough money to justify its owners in what then seemed to some of their contemporaries a rather hazardous investment in unnecessary luxury."[27] That the *Times* could afford such a move at this time was a point of curiosity not lost on the rival *Herald*, which explained Raymond's solvency as the result of stock improprieties.[28] Close scrutiny by its competitors notwithstanding, a year later the building at 41 Park Row was ready for occupancy and the *Times* wrote a glowing review of its accomplishment: "The first thing that attracts attention is the beautiful Stone of which the building is constructed. It is of a light olive color,—about equally removed from the glaring white of marble and the heavy dark hue of brownstone, which has hitherto been so generally used for building purposes,—and is in every respect decidedly superior to them both . . . [it] is capable of the highest style of ornamentation, and in all respects is certified, by the best judges, to be decidedly the best building material ever introduced into the City or country."[29]

New York Times Building, Thomas R. Jackson, 1858. (Picture Collection, The New York Public Library, Astor, Lenox and Tilden Foundations)

The elegant olive stone building was five stories high, still a commanding height on Park Row in the 1850s. Though the building had three main façades, the Park Row and Spruce Street fronts were more impressively ornamented since they were the most visible, and all fronts displayed "THE NEW YORK TIMES" signs in large gilt lettering. The ground level on all sides was colonnaded with stone piers in a continuous row of thirteen arches for windows and entrances, "resting on iron fluted pillars with Corinthian capitals."[30] The first floor contained the public areas, including the publication office, the business department, cashier, advertising clerk, and subscription clerk. To convey the classicism of the newspaper to the visiting public, these offices were decadently furnished in rich wood molding and marbles, and on the wall behind the counter were "medallions of Faust and Franklin." *Frank Leslie's Illustrated Newspaper* claimed that, though only five stories tall, the building's "height of upwards of eighty feet . . . elevates it above all surrounding buildings," and found it to be "a noble structure . . . complete in all its appointments."[31] Though not spectacular in its height, it was deemed serious, elegant, and well composed, like the newspaper it housed. Its olive green color was to the extremes of white marble and brown stone what the *Times* was to the scandal papers and the financial journals; it was comfortably and respectably in the middle, and "decidedly superior to them both." Though the expense seemed capricious and unnecessary to some, it served, at least in its own estimation, the purpose of establishing a solid foundation for the paper in the public mind. As Meyer Berger describes, "It was the handsomest newspaper structure of its day. Tradition had called for dull, faded, wheezy housing for daily journals, but . . . it was one of Gotham's show places. Other publishers thought Jones and Raymond slightly mad and figured that the building's cost might ruin them. It worked out quite the other way. It was excellent promotion and started a new trend in newspaper building architecture."[32]

When Raymond died at the age of forty-nine in 1869, the paper was left to his original partner George Jones. The news and business orientation of the *Times* seemed not to be adversely affected by the Jones takeover, and with a financial leader as editor, the paper was able to further differentiate itself from the crusading personal journalism of its rivals.[33] Jones hired George Browne Post, who had been a protégée of Richard Morris Hunt, to design a new home for the *Times*, in response to the attention that Hunt's *Tribune* tower had been taking away from the *Times*'s demure granite structure for the previous decade. Post was to architecture in the 1880s what Hunt had been the 1870s: the most sought-after and popular person for large commercial

commissions. He had won the commission for the Western Union Building, was the consulting architect on the Equitable Life Assurance Building
(1868–70)—two of New York's "proto-skyscrapers"—and was well known as
an innovator of tall elevator buildings in the French Second Empire style.

Though the *Times* structure still had the commanding location on the
three-fronted corner on Park Row, directly across Spruce Street onlookers
could not help but notice the *Tribune*'s "brick and mortar giraffe."[34] As *New
York Times* historian Elmer Davis wrote, "The building which in 1857 had
seemed preposterously expensive and unnecessarily large for a newspaper
office was by this time too small."[35] Rather than move to a new location, Post
built a skyscraper on top of the existing building. The feat of constructing
a new building on the same site while simultaneously removing the old one
dominated the coverage of the new Times tower, and it served to reinforce
the impression of the *Times* as a serious, business-minded organization that
would let nothing stand in the way of its primary duty of publishing a
newspaper, even the removal of its own office. The paper did not boast of
its new building until it was open and occupied by new tenants, explaining
its relative silence on the construction as modesty:

> If the *Times* has heretofore been sparing of words in praise and exposi-
> tion of its new building it was not because the public did not find in the
> structure an occasion of interest or the newspaper a source of pride.
> There has been justifying reason, no doubt, for frequent and laudatory
> comment upon the progress of this work, as unique in the manner of
> its doing as it is beautiful in its result, but the *Times* has observed that
> pretty much everybody in town and many in other towns were talking
> of the building, and it felt that a modest silence as to its own undertak-
> ings would not be considered, in the circumstances, a censurable failure
> to print the news. . . . Albeit the *Times* is little given to the practice of
> "blowing its own horn" it frankly admits a just pride in the superb house
> it has built for itself, and makes no apology for inviting its readers to share
> in its rejoicings. The *Times* Building, unsurpassed in the city in respect
> to beauty of architecture as it is unrivalled in altitude, is perhaps a more
> enduring and satisfactory evidence of prosperity than the most audacious
> monument ever erected by the arduous toil of the affidavit maker.[36]

Despite the *Times* professed aversion to self-promotion, the unstable
status of the newspaper under George Jones made a bold statement of fortitude a sound business decision. At thirteen stories, the new Times Building
was taller than any of its immediate neighbors, and as it occupied the same

Enlarged New York Times Building, April 29, 1889. (*New York Times*)

plot of land as its old building, it shared its advantages of being set off on its own block surrounded by plenty of open space. But the construction of the new building was not motivated by the need for more space, since while the new building was thirteen stories versus the previous five, the paper did not occupy more than five stories in the new structure. The presses were kept in the same location in the basement, and did not move or cease to run during the construction process. The main floors were kept for the public business operations, and the editorial and composing rooms were moved to the top two floors of the new building just as they had been in the old. In between, the new building provided eight floors of rental space.

Many contemporary reviewers found the final design confusing and cluttered, with too many pattern disruptions from the base to the top.[37] But as Montgomery Schuyler noted in *Architectural Record*, Post's design for the *New York Times* was an architectural translation of the Aristotelian principle that all forms should have a beginning, middle, and end. In this way the structure articulates the skyscraper elements of base, shaft, and capital (though with much more ornamental flourish than would later become standard in the tall buildings of modernists like Louis Sullivan and Frank Lloyd Wright).[38] For a newspaper building, this conscious adaptation of narrative structure added yet more layers of meaning to the design as a corollary to the structure of newspaper stories.[39] Other features of the building were used to extol the virtues of the newspaper, including the solid-steel-frame construction of the floors, noted for their endurance and strength,[40] and the absence of front door locks, because "the building will always be open, as work in a great newspaper office never ceases."[41] But the clearest conflation of the form of the building with the function of the newspaper was in the serious exterior of olive granite that paralleled the somber grey pages of the paper. As *King's Handbook of New York* described: "Discreet, moderate, bold, vigorous, perfect in every detail of ornamentation, in moldings, in capitals, in gargoyles; so beautiful that it charms the naive and the refined, the ignorant and the most learned in art; the Times building is the New York *Times* in stone."[42]

That the building could not only provide a monument on the skyline that captured the tone and aspirations of its paper but also serve as a vehicle for uplift for those who encountered it was a tall order for any structure, but the *Times* was well satisfied by its achievement. So enamored was Jones of his new building that he had a sketch of it printed on all *Times* letterhead, and sent pictures of it to clients and colleagues. Allen Frank, of the Frank,

Kierman & Company advertising agency responded to the gift accordingly: "Allow me to thank you very much for the very handsome picture of the Times Building which I have just received. It will have a place in my private office where it will remind me, if it should be needed, that the *Times* must be at the top of my list whenever I give out advertisements."[43] E. Prentiss Bailey similarly replied to Jones: "Permit me very gratefully to acknowledge the receipt of the fine portrait of yourself and the equally coveted picture of the Times Building. Both now occupy very conspicuous positions on the walls of my modest Observer Building, and will have the attention of visitors of which they are worthy."[44]

The image of the building was used as an icon of the newspaper not only to the general public, but also to other businessmen as a way of fusing the prosperous and solid building with the enterprise it housed. Such "stationery vignettes" adorning letterhead, envelopes, and invoices that Robert Biggert has shown were dominant in the period between 1860 and 1920 "provided Americans a mirror of the rapidly changing industrial and commercial landscape that surrounded them."[45] They ensured that the image of a company's architecture was a constant accompaniment to all transactions and extended the public relations value of the building beyond its initial unveiling. The responses of the *Times*'s clients indicate that they understood the intended meaning of the buildings; to serve as an advertisement and calling card that put the *Times* at the front of mind for both clients and competitors.

Despite his best efforts, however, Jones's determination to build the greatest newspaper building in the world did not secure the future of the *New York Times*; his best laid public relations efforts would not survive him. Shortly after the building was completed, in August 1891, Jones's death left the paper in the hands of his heirs, who had little newspaper experience. An economic downturn, an ill-fated attempt to raise the price of the paper to three cents, and the lingering debt left from the $1.1 million building all compromised the paper's success.[46] In desperation Jones's sons sold their interest to a group of employees at the *Times*, but as the building was not included in the deal, the rental income from tenants continued to go to the sons rather than the paper. With no working capital to sustain the operation of the newsroom, and with competition for news now coming from millionaires like Joseph Pulitzer and William Randolph Hearst, the *Times* struggled to survive inside the majestic structure that announced its success to the world. It was not until Adolph Ochs, owner of the *Chattanooga Times*, rescued the paper in 1896, that it began to operate on solid ground once again.

While the Times Building may not have had the legacy that George Jones had hoped for, it did have a striking effect on the rest of Park Row. In the same year that the Times Building was completed, Joseph Pulitzer commissioned George Browne Post to build a headquarters for his *New York World* that would be even bigger. There was perhaps no greater monument to the status of the newspaper in urban life and nothing more antithetical to the Times Building than the structure that Pulitzer erected to hold his *World*, which he officially named the Pulitzer Building. Every aspect of this building, from its owner, to the newspaper it housed, its architect, its construction, its advertising campaign, and its final unveiling, epitomized gaudy spectacle in the last decade of the nineteenth century.

## New Public Spaces

The papers of the nineteenth century sought to connect their buildings and their printed product in the public mind by any means available, and as the architectural competition heated up along Park Row, so too did the activity outside. With their publication names embedded on their towers' façades, the *Times* and the *Tribune* were beacons on the skyline. Their prominence was enhanced by their situation on oddly shaped plots of land providing spacious approaches and emphasizing height. By adopting tower form, they could be seen "in the round," evoking the Renaissance towers of Italy used for observation, public address, and signaling purposes. Where bell towers had historically marked time or events—the beginning and end of the work day, Senate sessions, executions, or to call citizens to gather or warn of danger—clock towers similarly functioned as a centralized source of information, reference point, and landmark. The Tribune's tower incorporated a large illuminated clock that attracted attention and could be seen from both rivers, and that also featured "a curious attic-level balcony, placed much too high above the street to be used as a speaking platform but included perhaps as a symbol of a building from which public announcements and news were sent out to the city."[47] The paper was the place from which to learn about current events, to gather in moments of celebration and crisis—a place to look for guidance.

Inasmuch as each building was a singular advertisement for the newspaper within, in aggregate the buildings along Park Row did provide an important public amenity: public space for the live presentation and reception of news. While the façades of these showpiece buildings garnered a great deal of attention in the press and trade coverage at their completion, during critical moments the public would have encountered these buildings when they were covered up. In major announcements of the last quarter of the nineteenth century, news could come in the form of words on paper, extras shouted by newsboys, or images projected onto large canvases draped from the front of newspaper buildings along Park Row. Anticipating later developments in news tickers, zippers, and digital screens, these "live" uses of architectural façades moved the site of news off the page and outside of the newsroom.

Nineteenth-century newspapers could be extremely responsive to the immediacy of events, with the capacity to insert news flashes into an edition running on the presses in two minutes.[48] This, combined with the printing of several updated editions per day, in both morning and evening form, contributed to a near-constant production news. Yet even with this massive outpouring of paper, building façades were used to fill in the gaps between editions. Election nights were especially busy, but so were New Year's Eves, or boxing matches, boat races, shipping news, natural and man-made disasters, war news, or any other announcements with temporal reveals. As Thomas Elsaesser has argued, nineteenth-century citizens were voracious consumers of news: "They were as hungry for instantaneity, for simultaneity, and interactivity as we are today."[49] The lively and energetic presence of crowds in front of news bulletins is testament to this hunger.

The earliest bulletin boards used chalk against slate, prefabricated block letters, and handwritten messages on paper to post updates. Later, stereopticons projected messages, photographs, cartoons, maps, and anything else that could be drawn on glass and illuminated against a canvas screen. Crushing crowds gathered to read the bulletins were held back by rows of police on horseback attempting to keep passages open for traffic. So used to staring up at bulletin boards were New Yorkers at this time that editorial cartoons reminded city people not to misinterpret fellow citizens with their chins in the air as haughty; these were simply the so-called "Bulletin board fiends" with their necks stuck in that position. Police reports recorded a spate of thefts—pocket watches, wallets, and women's purses—by pickpockets taking advantage of distracted crowds before the boards.

The building façades on Park Row constructed a space of and for news; a geography of information that existed independently of each paper's effort, or the ebb and flow of news events. As each building issued simultaneous and competing messages (depending on the political persuasion of the paper

Watching the bulletin boards on Park Row, 1899. (Picture Collection, The New York Public Library, Astor, Lenox and Tilden Foundations)

and the efficiency of their telegraph operator), readers had a full menu of options and opinions to choose from in selecting their information input. If readers were not loyal to one paper's boards over another, the noise of the crowd in front of one board would effectively direct their attention there. Reactions to the posted news were rambunctious, to say the least, instantly registering approval or disapproval of what was being shown. Such news dissemination, animated by eager news consumers, is a mode of reception that resists easy classification. The crowd was not only receiving news; it was by turns requesting and rejecting it. As the *Times* wrote in 1872, "When 9 o'clock came the good people who had waited in the streets so patiently for some news regarding the Mayoralty grew restive, and repeatedly demanded something about Havemeyer and O'Brien." While they waited, "The crowd was kept in excellent humor by our special artist's cartoons of the leading incidents and advocates of Liberalism, which were executed on the spot."[50]

In a manner suggestive of early news customization, gatherers could select, filter, and discard their information just by moving between boards. During the 1872 election, it was reported, "the Greeleyites wandered . . .

from one bulletin board to the other in search of consoling news, but found none." Disappointed at the news they were receiving, they rejected the bulletins themselves: "When, shortly after 8 o'clock, the dispatch appeared on the *Sun* board, 'Grant's majority in Philadelphia, 42,000; in the State, 80,000,' the rage and disappointment of the mob was vented in such cries as 'Tear that down,' 'Take that in,' 'It's a lie,' Etc."[51]

The reciprocal relationship between the boards and the papers, whereby each served to promote the other, can be seen in the boost that enthusiasm at the boards gave to the price of extras and that readers could be seen standing before the boards *and* reading newspapers at the same time, comparing them against each other. One frequently finds news of the boards in the paper as well, as when the *Times* congratulated itself on paper for having "results displayed fully fifteen minutes earlier than upon any other bulletin in Newspaper Square."[52] Next-day descriptions of "how the news was received" did more than indicate the mood of the receivers; they reveled in the *mode* of reception.

Not to be overlooked is the auditory component of these events, with crowd members reacting with cheers or boos and acting as their own amplification system to relay the messages to those in the back of the crowd who were too far away to read the boards. As the *Times* reported of the 1892

Newspaper War
Bulletins, 1898.
(Library of Congress)

Grover Cleveland victory, "As soon as new figures were placed upon the boards a shout would arise from those nearest the bulletin only to be taken up by those in the rear and carried along down the row, across the park, and in every direction."[53] The *Sun* was more colorful in its description of a similar scene: "If 400 lunatic asylums had emptied their boarders into the lively lane, the result would have been the sigh of a lovesick maiden compared to the ear-tearing, nerve-wrecking, brain shattering shriek and roar that went on between 7 o'clock and midnight. The racket and rumpus was a maddening compound of sound from every conceivable noise-making device. Early in the afternoon Broadway and the side streets were full of fakirs, selling tin horns, buzzers, tin pans, rattle bones, children's drums—anything and everything that could produce noise. They were sold out before dark."[54]

Although the buildings were not erected with these purposes in mind, the ensemble of buildings produced a sort of enclosure, owing to the irregular pattern of the street. While the World, Sun and Tribune structures were flush along Park Row, the Times Building across Ann Street was set back from the rest of the street. Rounding out the space was the Western Union Building and the Post Office to the south. The effect was like that of an open-air amphitheater, containing and hemming in the crowd as it amplified sound echoing from surrounding walls. After a street-sweeping campaign in 1893 aimed at ridding public spaces of their street furniture, shoeshine boys, and other impediments to circulation, many permanent bulletin boards were taken down on Park Row. These were soon replaced with more temporary, yet equally spectacular, stereopticon shows that were cast on canvas draped over the front of buildings. At one of its first demonstrations, the *Times* wrote in 1895,

> In Printing House Square the crowd was the greatest, for there the arrangements made by the New York Times to flash the figures upon canvas were the most elaborate and satisfactory. An immense cloth was stretched across the face of the Times building, and in a large scaffold erected for the purpose beside the Franklin Statue were five stereopticon operatives with as many instruments, by which they were enabled to keep the people fully informed of the latest returns.
>
> The platform was connected with THE TIMES editorial rooms on the eleventh floor of the building by a wire down which the successive bulletins were sent as soon as they were received in the office. Within thirty seconds after their receipt in the editorial rooms the curious in the street read their contents on the canvas.[55]

Five stereopticons were in play at once, and for the first time ever, this display showed the *Times*'s advertisements between voting returns. Hearst's *New York Journal* was similarly pioneering in the art of news spectacle. During the 1896 election, despite Hearst's campaigns against the evils of the mutoscope, all manner of inventive electric technologies were used, projecting a map of the United States illuminated with two colors of lights, text, still images, movies, and "panoramascope" pictures.[56] Live bands were hired and, for those not present at the show, forty-foot fire balloons in either red or green were shot into the sky to announce that either Roosevelt or Van Wyck had won the governorship.

Another layer in this early interactive multimedia moment was provided by Elisha Gray's short-lived but nonetheless influential invention of the telautograph, a technological innovation that would later morph into the fax machine. The telautograph was "an instrument designed for reproducing writing, pictures, drawings or any other product of the pen by transmission over a telegraph wire."[57] Its first public demonstration was at the Chicago World's Fair of 1893, where it captured the attention of scientists, journalists, and fair-goers alike. It allowed anyone to be their own telegrapher, because it reproduced handwriting as written, obviating the need for a telegraph operator or Morse code. Because it delivered a message in the same hand as it had been sent, and left a copy of the message with both sender and receiver, it was considered superior to the telephone, and thought likely to dominate business transactions. Early predictions were that the telephone would be relegated to trivial use, as a Knoxville paper wrote, offering "respite from the horrors of the 'hello' machine."[58] Commentators could imagine a wide range of applications for this new machine, for its ability to both draw and write using the same instrument, as a witness at the White City explained: "A press reporter or correspondent may, by means of it, send to his journal a picture of a railroad accident, or of beautiful scenery or striking architecture. The likeness of a criminal can be sent to anyone who can etch a likeness and produce it, thus offering a valuable aid to police work."[59]

None of these revolutionary applications would come to pass, but for a short time the telautograph found practical use on the bulletin boards of Park Row. Despite being lauded for its capacity for private message transmission, it was in these very public demonstrations that it found fame. And as with so many other defunct media technologies, its use tells us a great deal about the function of writing and inscription at the turn of the century. As the *Sun* described the scene at the 1906 gubernatorial election:

Shortly after 6 o'clock the returns began to appear on the illuminated sheets. In front of the *Journal* and *Tribune* offices rough booths on stilts sheltered the stereopticons, and from the dark gap in front of each, strong beams of white light jumped across the heads of the crowd onto the canvas.

A third sheet flapped against the side of the bridge station. Across the illuminated front of it moved a jointed spider's leg of shadow, which left lines of script and figures in its trail. "This is a telautograph" the shadow stick spelled out time and again in the breathing space between bulletins.

The phantom pencil had a fascination for the crowd. It would suddenly poise at the upper left hand corner of the sheet then begin: "445 Elect. Dists. out of 1475 in Man and Bronx: Hearst, Hughes—"

Then the pencil would stop and waver back to insert the figures while the people watching it took in a quick breath of anticipation. The figures would then be scratched and a roar from the crowd would punctuate the last stroke of the ricocheting beam of black.[60]

Compared with any other moment of live news production, the use of stereopticons annotated by the telautograph had no rival. Fusing words, numbers, photographs, maps, cartoons, and spontaneous doodling, these different representational systems acting together made for a stunning live multimedia show that was instant, reciprocal, and entertaining. As with other new media technologies, it was infused with no small amount of magic, as the *Tribune* in 1909 reported: "The thousands watched, with close attention, the giant telautograph, that glided a mammoth pen across the white surface of the bulletin board, giving the news from every election district in the greater city with unfailing accuracy. The actions of the giant hand that guided the mammoth pen were almost uncanny, so natural was the stroke, yet with no visible signs of human agency to direct its work. Everybody expressed surprise and satisfaction at the rapidity with which the returns were flashed on the Tribune bulletin board."[61] This magic pen was gifted with "unfailing accuracy" and speed. It seemed natural, even as it was credited as a "giant hand," and yet with no sign of human agency. As an immediate and localized inscription device it solved for any distrust of the printed word; appearing in handwriting it was both more personal and trustworthy, in an age beset by anxiety that newsprint as a medium was too far removed from the identity of its author. While the telautograph operator's identity was unknown, his style of wielding the instrument served to convey personality and often humor: "At one time, when things seemed to be getting dull, he wrote: 'Tom Sharkey challenges the winner. Hoo-ray!' The crowd was immensely tickled. Then he sketched lemons and rocks and other paraphernalia of the campaign, all of which made an instant appeal."[62] A skilled user of the telautograph could provide no small amount of entertainment for the crowd. Using animation and annotation he could bring the information to life, rousing the crowd by using his pen to underscore, exclaim, or draw stars around salient data.

The postings on newspaper office façades were as much advertisements for the papers as their celebrated architecture, but in moments of major news announcements they merged rather than disaggregated the reading public. The tall buildings along Park Row were of course manifestations of an increasingly powerful media industry, but as a group they also constructed an important public space before them. The buildings' visibility was a clear sign of the commercial power of the press, but the buildings also enabled a tangible space in which the public was constituted. The concentration of newspaper *buildings*, in a period prior to the concentration of the newspapers themselves, established the media as the producers of a town square and commons, and the writing on its architecture ensured that the public sphere was no mere abstraction. If each paper had a public—a debatable hypothesis given the heterogeneity of the city in the nineteenth century—at City Hall Park these publics were necessarily intertwined. One could not help but see the competing messages on either side of the screen directly ahead. More likely, these diverse publics gathered there precisely because of the competing messages and the promised cacophony. Perhaps visitors did not arrive to see only the message they were predisposed to agreeing with, but to see a live spectacular of competing information. Like an open market or bazaar, where the customer is the beneficiary of diversity and timeliness of goods, the competition for the immediate attention of the public ensured that the reader could customize the experience, demand news in real time, and encounter information serendipitously. The copresence of multiple publics provided the occasion for opposing views to stand side by side.

With such focus on building façades, and the era of yellow journalism requiring ever greater efforts to gain public legitimacy, the use of architecture as a publicity tool only grew more intense. Where the *New York Times* favored sobriety, and the *Tribune* cosmopolitanism, Joseph Pulitzer's *World* would reorient the competition toward sheer spectacle. It would be taller, brighter, and shinier than any that had gone before, and it would lead his rivals to devise new strategies for survival.

# Nineteenth-Century Stories and Columns

There is room in this great and growing city for a journal that is
not only cheap but bright, not only bright but large, not only large
but truly democratic—dedicated to the cause of the people rather
than that of purse-potentates—devoted more to the news of the
New than the Old World—that will expose all fraud and sham, fight
all public evils and abuse—that will serve and battle for the people
with earnest sincerity.
—*New York World*, May 11, 1883

Joseph Pulitzer's first editorials were infused with rhetoric about the New
World and the Old World. As a Hungarian immigrant, the "New World" to
Pulitzer signaled not only his latest business venture, but also America, and all
of the spectacle and publicity that anything "New" could garner. When Pulitzer bought the *New York World* in 1883, he was rescuing a failing newspaper

Postcard of Greeley Square and Broadway, ca. 1920. (Author's collection)

that many had already written off as a lost cause. Manton Marble had run the paper successfully for many years as a solid Democratic paper, but after becoming disillusioned by the election of 1876 Marble sold it to a railroad syndicate. It was soon exchanged as part of a package deal and landed in the hands of Jay Gould, who thought it could be used to promote his own business interests, including the takeover of Western Union. However, Gould's reputation as a much reviled businessman kept the paper from being taken seriously. Though the paper was losing money and had negligible circulation, its one valuable asset—membership in the Associated Press—made it attractive to prospective buyers. Pulitzer paid Jay Gould $346,000 for the paper, and leased the building that housed it at 32 Park Row in April 1883.

Pulitzer's formula for success was to emphasize "readability, excitement and education."[1] Knowing that the most lucrative untapped readership would be found in the immigrant population, he published a paper that was brief and breezy in its tone, accessible to everyone, and that heralded the strength and integrity of the common man.[2] News was made out of the relentless attack on the power elite, what Pulitzer called the "snobocracy," presented in provocative headlines, and short, succinct sentences packed with active verbs. He insisted that his writers "be suggestive, by which he did not mean obscene but prolific in ideas for headlines, stories and slants."[3] In one of his most famous circulation-boosting stunts, Joseph Pulitzer convinced patriotic readers to donate money to pay for the base on which the Statue of Liberty would stand, publishing donors' names in the newspaper in return. Readers were so excited to see their name in the paper that over $100,000 was raised in contributions of typically less than one dollar. Capitalizing on the opening of the Brooklyn Bridge as a historical as well as a magnificent feat of engineering, the *World* publicized the event so much that riots ensued, with *World* reporters on hand to record yet another news event that they had largely created. These and hundreds of other campaigns in the name of public service led the *World* and its publisher into the kind of spectacular extravagances that characterized the close of the nineteenth century. Among them, perhaps the most ambitious was the design and construction of a new headquarters on Park Row that attempted to capture and propel the power, prestige, and showmanship of its owner.

Though the typography of its early pages did not approximate the screaming headlines of later tabloids, the paper's content increasingly focused on bizarre accidents, murders, fires, and natural disasters. The hyperbolic fear that modern urban life was perilous and full of random danger was an easily supportable worldview that sensationalist newspapers exploited to its fullest. The dangerous city revealed itself through endless stories that cast a curious and penetrating glance into the hazards of overcrowded tenements in the Five Points district, expanding warehouses and factories, and increasingly taller office buildings. The unpredictable and volatile condition of the modern city was documented in the endless fires, crumbling buildings, suicides and falls from the tops of tall structures, and underground gas explosions. These frequent and bizarre occurrences were all symptomatic of a city whose population and growth could be construed as out of control, where unseen danger and unwitting victims were ever present. In the first few years of Pulitzer's takeover, the *World* published hundreds of stories making spectacles out of the precarious fate of the built environment. In typical rapid-fire, double- and triple-decker headlines, the paper chronicled disasters as "Narrow Escapes from Death—Workmen Fall Over Each Other in a Rush Down the Fireman's Ladders"; "Crushed in a Rookery—Six Boys Buried by the Falling of an Old Building"; "Lighted up by Flames—An Immense Fire Destroys Property Worth over a Million—Four Buildings on Wooster Street and Over One Hundred and Fifty Half-Clad People Driven into the Streets and Given Temporary Refuge in the Station House"; "Six Lives Lost—A Whole Family Suffocated in a Downtown Building—Several Daring Rescues—A Fireman Misses His Footing on an Icy Ladder and Falls from the Fourth Story of the Building—Terrible Story of a Servant."

This new, machine-gun approach to news was instantly successful, aided by the fact that Pulitzer's *World* was being sold for two cents a copy, the cheapest paper in the field at the time. By September 1883, the other major papers had cut their prices to compete, which did more financial damage to them than it did to the *World*. Pulitzer boasted in lengthy editorials every time a rival paper lowered its price, a strategy that he correctly interpreted as a desperate sign of defeat. Pulitzer took equal delight in publishing his own circulation figures on the front page of his paper, which he did as soon as his were highest. When it was clear that other papers' circulation were not keeping up they tried quietly to stop publishing their figures in their pages. As each ceased this self-reporting Pulitzer drew attention to it in his own editorials as a further sign of his triumph.

Even as the fear-mongering content of the newspaper chronicled the deterioration and impermanence of city structures, Pulitzer vowed to create a building that would stand as the lasting testament to his and his newspaper's status in New York, a concrete beacon in the fragile city that his paper was documenting. His aim was to build as close to the Herald building as possible, understanding it to be his most formidable rival. As W. A. Swanberg describes, "He envisioned this not only as a personal victory over the lone New York newspaper publisher who still offered the *World* any challenge, but as a stroke of architectural publicity impressive to everyone."[4] When no land near the Herald could be procured, Pulitzer bought property on Park Row across Frankfort Street from the *New York Sun*. The opportunity to upstage the Herald in architectural dominance may have been lost, but the effect on the tiny Sun Building was even more extreme. The five-story rookery had already been significantly dwarfed by the Tribune tower that surrounded it—but Pulitzer's project would diminish them both. The degradation continued through construction, and according to one biographer, "every rising girder and stone in the new *World* building would be a noisy and visible humiliation to Dana [of the *Sun*], day after day and month after month."[5] For Pulitzer architecture was the weapon of choice in the newspaper wars, brandished mercilessly against rivals: "Even the shabby little building of the *Sun* will be benefited by the splendor of its neighbor. Yet the *Sun* dreads being overshadowed architecturally by the *World*, as it already has been overshadowed by us in circulation, influence, character, enterprise and all that makes a newspaper successful and powerful."[6]

With Richard M. Hunt acting in an advisory capacity in the competition, Pulitzer chose architect George B. Post, whose already solid reputation as a leading architect was further enhanced by his work on the New York Times Building three doors down. In choosing Post, Pulitzer sought to capitalize on his publicity value and his experience with the Times Building, though it was written into Post's contract that the World Building be "at least as good as that of the Times."[7] For all of Post's experience and prestige, however, Pulitzer was involved in the design of his building at every stage of development, and the two grandest gestures—the gold dome and the three-story entrance—were "originally and entirely Mr. Pulitzer's conception."[8]

Pulitzer's aim was to have the tallest building in the world and a shining beacon in New York City. It was his explicit instruction that "the structure must be in every sense an architectural ornament to the metropolis; that it must be a magnificent business structure of the first order, embodying the very latest and best ideas in constructive art; that, to be worthy of the paper it housed, it must also be the best equipped newspaper office in existence."[9] At twenty-six stories and rising 309 feet from the sidewalk to the base of the lantern on top of the dome, the building achieved the height superiority and the notoriety that Pulitzer wanted. The three-story arched front entrance was flanked, like the Tribune and Times Buildings before it, by "polished Quincy granite columns," which in turn were surrounded by "bulletin-boards of polished Hurricane Island granite" for posting the day's news. Classical allegorical sculptures ornamented the inside and the outside of the building: an Atlas carrying a globe stood in one corner of the rotunda of the publication office, and an "immense globe light, seventeen feet in diameter, showing the points of the compass" reinforced the "world" theme; these were the architectural companions to the paper's front page masthead vignette of two globes (showing two hemispheres) separated by the Statue of Liberty. Under the pediment at the top of the structure on the outside, four male supports represented the four human races. Above the large entrance were "bas-reliefs of heroic female figures of Justice and Truth, the one bearing her scales and a bronze sword, and the other rearing her torch."[10] Four female torchbearers in bronze stood on pedestals above the porch, each thirteen feet tall:

> The figures represent Art, Literature, Science and Invention, and the uplifted torches signify their mission of enlightenment to the *World*. The designs are most striking and artistic. . . . One needs a glass to appreciate the details of the torch-bearers from the street. Each figure is distinct in detail and posture. Art holds a palette in one hand and is kneeling on a capital. At the feet of Literature lies a scroll, while an open volume rests in her left hand. Science has her globe and Invention her appropriate symbols. They form a most artistically appropriate and architecturally satisfactory crown for the porch section of the facade.[11]

Despite the *World*'s own rhetoric about favoring the New World over the old, by the paper's own description, "architecturally speaking, the Pulitzer Building [wa]s of the Renaissance order, with a tendency to Venetian detail."[12] The building's exterior was to be an expression of the paper's principles and values, and in case these precepts were not self-evident, the Souvenir Supplement educated citizens on how to read the building as a monument to public service and uplift, to see the structure as a homily for daily life: "The People have built it. Neither editorial ability nor business sagacity has reared this splendid pile. Public confidence is its real foundation. Public favor is its real architect. 'Its every stone comes from the people, and represents public approval for public services rendered.' There is a sermon in these stones: a significant moral in this architectural glory. Fidelity to the

Pulitzer Building,
George B. Post, 1890.
(Milstein Division of
United States History,
Local History &
Genealogy, Picture
Collection, The New
York Public Library,
Astor, Lenox and
Tilden Foundations)

Public Welfare, fearless opposition to the Wrong and vigorous defense of
the Right, a persistent aspiring to loftier Ideals, are the lessons it teaches. It
lifts American journalism to a nobler plane."[13]

The $2.5 million cost of the building was only one in a string of superla-
tives associated with the structure, which also included having the highest
business elevator in the world. The Souvenir Supplement claimed that the
bricks used in the building could have built an entire town, that the structure weighed 68,000,000 pounds, and that there were two miles of wrought
iron columns.[14] But the building's most outstanding feature was surely its
gold dome, considered a cheap and tasteless spectacle for the masses by the
architectural critics of the day. Had its size and height not been enough, at
night the dome's ribs and lantern were illuminated. According to a New York
pictorial guide from the turn of the century, the gallery of the lantern was
open to visitors "at all times during the day, from which a wonderful view
could be obtained of the metropolis and environs for miles around."[15] The
shiny gold dome radiated over its territory. Since the construction of the

Tribune Building, the tall tower of newspaper offices had become a way of establishing a newspaper's sphere of influence, and hyperbolic statements of the distance of its reach served to emphasize the paper's dominion. Boasting about the views afforded from these new tall towers was one of the many ways that height was communicated through print. The *New-York Tribune* and the *New York Times* had already established the practice by regularly noting that nothing stood in the way of their purview of the city from the top of their buildings, with the *Times* adding in 1889 that it was "on fairly familiar terms with the clouds."[16] These unsubtle jabs at neighbors kept the competition alive among newspapers and reinforced height supremacy as an index of the occupant's success, but Pulitzer was equally proud of the view *of* his dome: "It is the first glimpse of New York that the ocean voyager gets. The traveler coming down the Sound sees its outlines towering above everything else against the southern sky. From Jersey's shores, from Brooklyn Heights, from the beach of Staten Island, from points far remote it is first discerned as one approaches New York looming above the busy metropolis, above Trinity's lofty spire, above the tall towers and high roofs of its neighbors—a giant among giants."[17] That there were other giants in the skyscraping newspaper field was a fact notably absent in the *World Almanac* published annually by the *World*. On its "Height of Prominent Buildings" list in 1895, Pulitzer's building is the lone entry among newspapers.

The advertising campaign for tenants of the Pulitzer Building took full advantage of the saleable commodity of height, and in the month leading up to the building's official opening the *World* mounted a comprehensive campaign to attract good tenants to it. The campaign stressed the healthful benefits of light and air that were achieved by such a tall building, its structural integrity, and the publicity value of such a distinct design, all articulated within the organizing principle of the visual. An ad from September 7, 1890, announced that the building was open for viewing, and emphasized the lighting, ventilation, location, and affordability of the building for offices. On September 9 and 10, the ads used Pulitzer's reliable categories of "old" and "new" to describe the merits of his new building over any other old building. On the first day the ad depicts an unhappy man alone in an old office with plaster falling off the walls; on the second day he is seen relocated in the new *World* Building in the lap of luxury. The text claims that "it will not only attract new patrons, but because of the light, pure air and magnificent outlook will give you and your clerks better health and spirits, making it possible to do more work in less time and with less fatigue." The following

# The Old and the New.

**SCENE I.—THE OLD.**

Any man can afford to have a GOOD office, or, to put it in another way, no man can afford to have a POOR office.

A GOOD office is one conveniently located in regard to facilities for transportation, and should be in a building the location of which is well known. It must be properly ventilated, perfectly lighted and during Winter comfortably heated, and at all times clean and attractive.

Such an office will preserve your health and bring you new patrons.

The difference in rent between a good office and a poor one will be a very small percentage on the increase in your business.

Everybody knows the location of the PULITZER BUILDING, the future home of the New York WORLD.

There is but one other spot on earth where so many people pass regularly daily.

It has every advantage that an office building could possess.

The rents are moderate and cover electric lighting, heating and cleaning.

# The Old and the New.

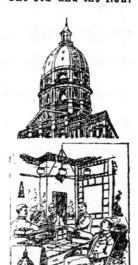

**SCENE II.—THE NEW**

The man who does not increase his business by having an office in the PULITZER BUILDING will be one who has all the business that he wants. It will not only attract new patrons, but because of the light, pure air and magnificent outlook will give to you and your clerks better health and spirits, making it possible to do more work in less time and with less fatigue.

Three passenger elevators are given up entirely to the use of tenants. The moderate rent covers everything—electric lighting, heat and cleaning. There are no "extras."

On the side towards the Bridge are offices with a steady north light, perfectly suited to Architects.

The offices will be ready for occupancy in October. They can be inspected now.

The light is not obliged to struggle into the offices via a well that Old Sol has never seen. Every office has direct daylight from the outside. The building towers so much above all surrounding structures that nothing can obstruct either light or air.

But why not see all this for yourself? The building is now open and the Superintendent, who can be found on the premises forenoons, between 8 and 12 (3d floor, room 8), will show offices and give terms. Tenants can move in next month.

The moderate rates cover heating, electric lighting and cleaning. There are no "extras."

An important consideration is the fact that the PULITZER BUILDING will be the best-known building in town.

☞ OVER 25 per cent. of the offices are already taken.

Ads for the new Pulitzer Building, published September 7–10, 1890, in the *New York World.*

Hundreds of thousands of eyes will be turned daily towards the PULITZER BUILD-ING. Its dome and upper stories can be seen from almost every point in New York, Brooklyn, Jersey City, Staten Island and from both rivers and the bay. In fact, there can hardly be found a spot for 20 miles about from which it cannot be seen.

An object constantly in the eye is constantly in the mind. If you have an office in the PULITZER BUILD-ING and make it known, you will be in mind, too. In consequence your patronage will constantly increase.

The building is open daily to inspection.

*Address or apply personally forenoons, between 8 and 12, to the Superintendent, on the premises (3d floor, room 8), Park Row.*

Over 25 per cent. of the offices are already taken.

*All will be ready for occupancy next month.*

day the campaign turned toward building integrity, illustrating that the building was immune from the rampant fires the newspaper had been scrupulously documenting for the past several years, exclaiming that prospective tenants "can laugh at the Fire Fiend . . . in the Pulitzer Building. No blaze can enter from without and none can spread through floor or wall within." The final two ads give the notion of spectacle double meaning: the September 15 ad shows several pairs of spectacles suspended above text that read: "You don't need these in the Pulitzer Building, every office has direct daylight from the outside. The building towers so much above all surrounding structures that nothing can obstruct either light or air." The following day the building was shown surrounded by dozens of little eyes, and the text claimed that "hundreds of thousands of eyes will be turned daily towards the Pulitzer Building. . . . An object constantly in the eye is constantly on the mind." This campaign emphasizing the visual aspects of the building is made somewhat ironic by the fact that by the time the building was finished Pulitzer himself had lost most of his sight.

On the day of the building's unveiling, the public was invited to come and see the new attraction. Governor David B. Hill of New York, State Secretary Chauncey Depew, William C. Whitney, and Thomas Edison all gave speeches, but none was more immortalized or so often repeated than Pulitzer's own words of dedication:

God grant that this structure be the enduring home of a newspaper forever unsatisfied with merely printing news—forever fighting every form of Wrong—forever Independent—forever advancing in Enlightenment and Progress—forever wedded to truly Democratic ideas—forever aspiring to be a Moral Force—forever rising to a higher plane of perfection as a Public Institution. . . .

> Let it be ever remembered that this edifice owes its existence to the
> public; that its architect is of popular favor; that its moral cornerstone is
> Love of Liberty and Justice; that its every stone comes from the people
> and represents public approval for public services rendered.[18]

The speech was reprinted in the *World* over several days, and in most of
the *World*'s publicity material and anniversary publications. More than any
other statement by a newspaper publisher, Pulitzer's words directly fuse the
form and function of the newspaper with that of the building, maintaining
the newspaper-as-structure metaphor throughout his speech to emphasize
the public nature (and by implication the public good) in both. On opening
day, wrote journalist Allen Churchill,

> Most of the citizens gazing in awe at the gold dome were afraid to go up
> to the inside of the *World* Tower, though elevator rides on that jubilant
> day were free to all. Tough-minded Ballard Smith, veteran of many rug-
> ged news stories, was actually afraid to look out the windows of the dome
> and could not summon nerve to do so for nearly a year. The Reverend
> Dr. Parkhurst, that notable crusader against vice, was one of those who
> dared take the elevator ride to the top, where he offered doubtful tribute
> by saying that when looking out the windows he felt like Christ being
> tempted by the Devil on the Mount. Still, it was an unnamed citizen who
> won ad-lib honors of the day. Stepping off the elevator on the top floor,
> he crystallized the event perfectly by loudly demanding "Is God in?"[19]

The building was "Pulitzer's 20-story shout of triumph over his rivals, the
structural equivalent of the *World*'s steady self-advertisement" according to
Swanberg.[20] As a large-scale public display designed as an object of public
curiosity, the Pulitzer Building achieved in masonry what the *World* had with
paper. The paper and the building were solid and credible in an unstable
and unfamiliar urban landscape, and the feat of wonder that this skyscraper
demonstrated paralleled the aesthetic thrill of urban space and its represen-
tation in the newspaper.

## Inventing Herald Square

The escalating competition between Pulitzer and Hearst led James Gordon
Bennett Jr. to contemplate a move that would signal the beginning of the end
of the Park Row: he decided to move his *Herald* uptown. There was much
to be gained by this separation in Bennett's view. It would demonstrate to

readers that the *Herald* was "above" the cheap and vulgar scandal papers, by literally placing the paper higher uptown. By following a demographic shift north, the *Herald* could claim to be staying closer to an "uptown" readership, further distinguishing itself from the other papers. It would also be a move away from City Hall and Wall Street in an era vexed by allegations that newspapers were being controlled by politicians and financiers. To get outside of the concentrated newspaper fray at Park Row could have a useful purifying effect, especially seen against the *Sun's* move to the former Tammany building. As a pioneer in a relatively undiscovered part of town, the paper could also profitably take advantage of more moderate land values, and take credit for the development of a whole new area.

All of these considerations factored into Bennett's decision to move north, but people in the newspaper business knew that the move was further precipitated by Pulitzer's garish dome nearby. In response to what he deemed the "ostentatious bad taste" of the World Building, Bennett "would house his *Herald* in a building which would be a model of architectural beauty."[21] When correspondent Ralph D. Blumenfeld called on Bennett in Paris in 1890, it was to discuss newspaper business, but as Blumenfeld later wrote in his diary, "The only reference to business during the journey was a remark about Joseph Pulitzer, whose *World* in New York ha[d] been making a lot of noise and money. 'Poor, misguided, selfish vulgarian. Can't last,' was all he would say. 'He's going to put up a skyscraper of fourteen or fifteen stories. We'll put up one of two floors, just to show how it should be done.'"[22]

Bennett purchased a trapezoidal plot of land bound by Broadway, Sixth Avenue, and Thirty-Fifth and Thirty-Sixth Streets. The property had been the home of the Seventy-First Regiment Armory, which the *Times* reported "would of course, make way for a skyscraper," apparently unaware of Bennett's plans.[23] Bennett's disdain for the garish Pulitzer Building directly influenced not only the location but also the design of his new structure: a graceful, low, public building to mark a decisive departure from the current vogue of ever-taller newspaper buildings. Bennett commissioned Stanford White, of the legendary McKim, Mead and White architectural firm to design the new Herald Building uptown. The firm had a growing reputation for opulent Renaissance domestic architecture, and was the most sought after for the growing class of millionaires in New York. White had already renovated the interior of the Broadway and Ann building, as well as designing the interior of Bennett's yacht, the *Namouna*. In the late 1880s and 1890s, the firm was also establishing an unprecedented reputation for important civic monuments. Beyond Madison Square Garden, they had completed the Boston Public Library, the University Club, and Columbia University's Low Library, in addition to building the agricultural pavilion and the New York State pavilion at the World's Columbian Exposition in Chicago in 1893. But McKim, Mead and White were not skyscraper architects; they built large, imposing and important structures that commanded attention with their historically exacting Renaissance styling and monumental scale. They designed elemental features of the urban landscape—including lampposts, statues, and the majestic arch at Washington Square—that became signposts in helping to make order out of unruly city space. They were oriented toward ensemble buildings that were massive and yet relatively low, emphasizing public values and accessibility. For Bennett, these were all principles on which the *Herald* was founded. If the *Herald* was to be embedded into the very fabric of the city, there was no better way than to use the architects responsible for building so many of the celebrated characteristics of the built environment of New York. The firm's work at Chicago's White City fit well with the propensity toward exhibition initiated by James Gordon Bennett Sr., and in choosing architects better known for their domestic and civic designs than their commercial ones, Bennett Jr. could reorient the paper away from the crass commercialism of his rivals.

As Bennett Jr. had suspected, commerce did follow him north and the area became a popular location for theaters, department stores, and hotels. That his move was closely followed by Macy's Department Store to the adjacent corner on 34th Street helped to solidify his connection to an upscale consumerist readership while keeping a reliable advertiser close at hand. As spectacles of turn-of-the-century tourism and consumerism, the intersection of the Herald Building and Macy's became an essential destination.

Bennett Jr. requested of White a building based on the Doge's Palace in Venice, but White refused because the National Academy of Design was already based on this building, and White found it insufficiently classical.[24] The architect and client compromised on a design based in the Loggia of the Palazzo del Consiglio in Verona, built by order of the Venetian Republic in 1497. The resulting building was a very long two-story structure arcaded by six white columns at ground level on the front and twenty each on the long sides, inviting people to approach the building from all directions. Inside the archways were large sheets of plate glass that allowed for views down into the presses in the basement, making a public spectacle out of the production of the newspaper, and revealing what had been hidden

Herald Building, McKim, Mead and White, 1895. (Picture Collection, The New York Public Library, Astor, Lenox and Tilden Foundations)

in all other newspaper buildings. A clock and a wind direction instrument distinguished the front façade over the doorway, flanking an American flag, above which a large bell with two mechanical bell-strikers stood, and at regular intervals along the roofline were twenty bronzed owls.[25] Though not made of marble, the new Herald Building had a similar exterior to its previous marble palace, with the new one covered instead in yellow and white terracotta. And like its previous home, this new Herald Building borrowed liberally from styles most associated with bank architecture. The entrance lobby was perfectly circular and majestic, with the gratuitous use of space that normally only banks and insurance companies could afford. Like the museums and department stores that Bennett Sr. had sought to emulate for their impeccable categorization of artifacts, order was achieved in this new building with symmetry, repetition, and display.

The Herald Building was enthusiastically received in the popular press and in guidebooks as a marvel of Renaissance classicism in midtown Manhattan. The trade magazine *The Journalist* wrote that the building "breathes independence, and bears upon its face the stamp of enterprise, ambition and foresight," that it was "a monument to the wisdom of James Gordon Bennett."[26] *Harper's Weekly* reported excitedly that "nothing in the career of James Gordon Bennett so accurately expresses his leadership of uncommercial journalism as the beautiful Italian palace at the junction of Broadway and Sixth Avenue which was occupied by the New York *Herald* on August 20th. This is his reply to the newspaper proprietors who have erected giant office buildings, in which the editorial forces occupy garrets and the pressmen are crowded into dark cellars. Architecturally, the new home of the *Herald* is a rebuke to the utilitarianism of the American metropolis, an appeal for something better than skyscraping ugliness."[27] As a most poignant exception that proved the rule, the new building made it possible for the *Herald* to communicate independence, strength, and self-reliance by moving away from Park Row, and to convey noncommercialism, even selflessness, by not building a skyscraper. That "uncommercial journalism" was a contradiction in terms seemed not to diminish the achievements of the new structure.

Those toiling inside, however, did not share the popular opinion of the new structure. What seemed like an ideal situation, with proximity to the terminals of the Pennsylvania and Long Island Railroads and the promise of a subway system that would find its way underneath Broadway in coming years, the building seemed perfectly poised as a circulation and distribution hub. But the street-bound island that the building was on made it difficult for paper delivery trucks to approach the building, and made it impossible to expand in size as the paper grew. According to Richard O'Connor, to insiders it was known as the Commodore's Folly: "the composing room was located under the hip-roof and was abominably hot and cramped, particularly in the summertime."[28]

Its inconveniences notwithstanding, the Herald Building was a stroke of genius for the floundering newspaper. O'Connor deemed it not only beautiful but adding "to the Bennett prestige just when he needed it, and it attracted tourists with its huge plate glass windows opening into the pressroom under the arcade."[29] Whether by design or default, Bennett Jr. framed his move as a sign of his commitment to his readers, making him appear more attuned to the demographic shifts in the city than his competitors. His geographic removal from Park Row effected a symbolic separation from the philistinism of the downtown newspapers, political machines, and money swindlers. By erecting a low building, he was able to appear less greedy and more sincere than the other papers, despite the fact that it was mainly his dislike of tenants that led him to the two-story design. As *World* journalist Don Seitz later remarked in his biography of the Bennetts, "where Pulitzer had aimed to touch the skies, Bennett kept close to the earth."[30] His transplant took root so successfully that his intersection became permanently known as Herald Square.

Crowd Watching "Play-o-graph" World Series 1911 at Herald Building. (George Grantham Bain Collection, Library of Congress)

Despite its relatively low height, the Herald Building at 34th Street was no less a site of public gathering in its day. Crowds appeared on a regular basis to view its presses through the large windowed bays, and on special occasions it could command enormous crowds to the square. Primary among these was baseball's World Series, which the *Herald* celebrated with the inventive use of the Play-o-graph. Like the telautograph before it, the Play-o-graph connected distant events via telegraph to the visual display of information on the façade of a newspaper building. Here, a wooden baseball diamond stood just in front of the building, and when each play was made, operators working behind the board would move the ball over the field to correspond to the action at the stadium.[31] Between 1911 and 1913, nineteen games were recreated in this manner, drawing crowds, by the paper's own estimate, of 30,000 to 40,000 people. In 1914 the same space was used for bulletins and stereopticons showing news of the European war, congesting traffic along Broadway and requiring the presence of police to maintain order.[32] The *Herald*'s move uptown and away from the gathering grounds at City Hall Park did not diminish its ability to make a newspaper building a destination for the reception of news—but the *New York Times* was soon to shift the center of media gravity irrevocably to 42nd Street.

## New York Times Square

It was clear that the *Herald*'s move to 34th Street and Broadway had signaled an important moment in the newspaper industry when the *New York Times* announced their plans to move even farther north to the intersection of Broadway, Seventh Avenue, and 42nd Street. The competition for height supremacy on Park Row had not favored the *Times* since Pulitzer's World Building overtook it in 1890. The *Tribune* had responded by removing its clock tower, adding nine more stories, and replacing the tower, making it taller than the World. As the *Times* reported: "The *Tribune* Association is to add a skyscraper to the Printing House Square neighborhood by increasing the height of its building from ten to nineteen stories. The *Tribune*'s home was known from the first as the 'Tall Tower,' and when it is more than 100 feet higher than it is now it will have the distinction of being . . . a landmark visible within a radius of twenty five miles from City Hall."[33]

In 1903, George Post's 1888 Times building was similarly enlarged by removing the mansard roof and replacing it with five new stories at the top of the structure. The thirteen-story structure was originally to have seventeen stories, with the additional stories first proposed in 1896. However, by the time the project was completed, the *Times* had already decided to build an entirely new building.[34] One can imagine that had time-lapse photography been available, the rooflines of the Park Row in these years would have looked something like a game of leapfrog. Whenever fortunes allowed (or publicity demanded), new floors could be added to give substance to the conflated claims of "tallest" and "most successful." When the *Herald* and *Times* moved off the street, the game took on a new dimension. The *New York Times* responded by both moving uptown *and* building taller.

The *Times* had been under new management since 1896, when Adolph Ochs rescued the paper from George Jones's incapable heirs. The paper was then bankrupt and had a circulation of only 9,000. As Arthur L. Sulzberger wrote, "It was losing [money] at the rate of a thousand dollars a week. Its presses were rusty and tired, and its staff was hopelessly discouraged. Reporters on other newspapers thought it amusing that a Tennessee yokel should think he could save it."[35] Many historians have noted the parallels in the

Construction of the Times Building at 42nd Street, ca. 1903.
(Author's collection)

atmosphere into which Henry J. Raymond and Ochs emerged. Both reasoned that in the increasingly debased climate of newspaper sensationalism, people would welcome a serious and straightforward paper that would simply and reliably report the news. The similarity can also be seen in their reaction to the success that both enjoyed with the *New York Times:* both sought new structures to house the growing operation, and both extended the somber and serious tone of the newspaper into the architecture of its buildings.

Adolph Ochs's takeover of the *New York Times* was arguably the most significant event in the paper's history, and historians of the paper date its inception from 1896 almost as often as they do from 1851. On August 16, 1896, Ochs printed the most famous mandate in American newspaper history:

To undertake the management of the New-York *Times*, with its great history for right-doing, and to attempt to keep bright the lustre which Henry J. Raymond and George Jones have given it, is an extraordinary task. But if a sincere desire to conduct a high-standard newspaper, clean, dignified and trustworthy, requires honesty, watchfulness, earnestness, industry and practical knowledge applied with common sense, I entertain the hope that I can succeed in maintaining the high estimate that thoughtful, pure-minded people have ever had of the New-York *Times*. It will be my earnest aim that the New-York *Times* give the news, all the news, in concise and attractive form, in language that is parliamentary in good society, and give it as early, if not earlier, than it can be learned through any other reliable medium; to give the news impartially, without fear or favor, regardless of any party, sect, or interest involved; to make the columns of the New-York *Times* a forum for the consideration of all questions of public importance, and to that end to invite intelligent discussion from all shades of opinion.[36]

Ochs maintained the *Times*'s policy of editing a clean, family-oriented newspaper. This meant avoiding gossip and scandal, and carefully scrutinizing the orientation of advertisers, even refusing the ads from what he considered disreputable companies. In a famous instance he refused a political advertisement from Tammany, continuing the tradition of crusading against the political machine that had begun with Raymond and was continued by Jones. He started the review of books and the Sunday magazine, and created a space for letters to the editor. The rebirth of the *New York Times* owed a great deal to Ochs's new initiatives, which helped to draw readers away from the Pulitzer's *World* and Hearst's *Journal* as well as from the more costly financial papers. He expanded the business section by developing a daily listing of all the individual merchants that were in town on business and what they were in the market for, making the paper indispensable to both local and foreign traders. The look of the paper was altered as well, according to Meyer Berger: "He banished most of the agate type—fine, small letters—from news stories, widened the space between lines of type and shortened column rules to lessen the strain on the old presses. He bought better newsprint and ink to obtain sharper reproduction, threw out standing ads that returned next to no revenue and were eyesores, and started using datelines on important stories originating outside New York."[37] As the paper became more stable financially, Ochs added staff and invested in better printing technology, and in eight years was in a position to build one of the most significant newspaper buildings in the city.

Ochs knew that an impressive architectural statement could accomplish the necessary public and community relations that a newspaper required, because he had performed a similar feat at his *Chattanooga Times* several years earlier. Constructed two years after Pulitzer's World Building, Ochs's building appeared to have been greatly influenced by Pulitzer's design, as Berger describes: "In 1892, with characteristic business daring, Ochs completed the handsomest newspaper plant in the South and filled it with the newest machinery at a total cost of around $150,000, almost all of it bank-borrowed money. Chattanooga was inordinately proud of the lovely gold-domed edifice. When the plant was opened on the night of December 7, 1892, more than 10,000 persons rode in to gasp at it. Chattanooga's foremost clergymen, bankers and merchant leaders talked for hours of Ochs' tremendous contribution to the community, and gave him a handsome grandfathers clock."[38]

When a new Times building was deemed necessary, Ochs initially sought out the land on Broadway that would eventually be the site of the Woolworth Building. But according to Alan Churchill, "when this deal fell through, he was not disappointed": "For having thought seriously about the future of New York, Ochs joined his eccentric colleague James Gordon Bennett—with whom he agreed in no other way than this—in realizing that the trend in New York was strongly northward, he also came to the conclusion, says a biographer, 'that Park Row was dying, just as old persons must die.'"[39]

For Ochs, the decision to move uptown was not nearly as risky as it had been for the *Herald*, given that the subway system was finally being built, and that its main interchange was being developed at 42nd Street. As the *Times* explained in the article reporting the move, "To many of the older New Yorkers, the notion of a newspaper moving so far up town will seem singular. For years, the popular idea has been that location near the City Hall Park, where so many newspapers are now grouped, was an essential. This was true in the years gone by, and is still true in great measure. The next eighteen months, however, promise to make a revolution in many respects, owing to the new transit facilities which the underground railway will provide."[40] By the time Ochs made his decision to purchase the trapezoidal piece of land at Broadway and Seventh Avenue on Longacre Square (that would quickly become known as Times Square),[41] the sites in the city at which Broadway intersected with an avenue were becoming very desirable properties for newspaper companies. The *Herald* had already relocated to the intersection of Broadway and Sixth Avenue, and William Randolph Hearst had plans to move his *Journal* to the next one north, at Columbus Circle and the intersection of Broadway and Eighth Avenue.[42]

Ochs chose architects Cyrus Eidlitz and Andrew C. MacKenzie. Eidlitz was responsible for the New York Bar Association Building on West 44th Street, the Bank for Savings in Gramercy Park, St. George's Episcopal Church on East 16th Street, and the renovations on St. Peter's Episcopal Church in the Bronx, built by his father Leopold. This expertise in church architecture was significant for the Gothic-inspired structure built for the *Times* at Times Square. In fact, Sara Landau and Carl Condit argue that it was the Times Building, and not the usually credited Woolworth Building, that initiated the Gothic skyscraper in New York.[43] The adaptation of this ecclesiastical form in the Woolworth Building led many commentators to draw conclusions about the replacement of religion by commerce, but few made such statements about the use of this iconography by press buildings, which had, for the past half century, been aspiring in architecture to overtake church spires on the horizon to convey the prominence of the press over religion. According to the *Times* Building Supplement, the Gothic style was used because

> it was plain from the first that with so irregular a ground plan the classical styles did not supply the precedents needed and that classical and formal symmetry would have to be abandoned in favor of picturesque irregularity. The free and romantic styles and periods of architecture were, so to say, "indicated" by the conditions of the problem. Of these styles, Gothic is of course by far the most important and the most fruitful in precedents available for modern uses. The choice of Gothic for the style of the Times Building was accordingly not capricious, but proceeded from a consideration of the particular requirements of this building.[44]

Although the *Times* easily rationalized the Gothic style as the most functional alternative for the needs of the building, it did also not resist the celestial connotations that the style suggested:

> As the eye lifts from base to summit of that lofty tower the wonder grows. The immediate sense of great height, joined to the sense, not less immediate, of uncommon slenderness and grace, implants the belief that one is confronted by some public commemorative edifice, by a tower erected as a civic adornment, or by an imposing fragment of architecture that, like the Tour St. Jacques, has in some way got detached from its ecclesiastical or municipal pile, a notion which leads instinctively to a quest for the

belfry. At once and convincingly the impression of non commercial use is deepened by the unusual and tender color of the walls.[45]

Architectural historians have provided contesting interpretations of the Gothic style, many of which make the *Times*'s own readings—as either dictated by the site or the functionality of the organization—less convincing. Umberto Eco recalls that the Gothic evokes "the vault of Celtic forests, and thus the pre-Roman world, barbaric and primitive, of druidical religiosity" allowing that the form has over time "been able to connote diverse things."[46] For the *Times*, the appropriation of religious symbolism could communicate both participation and stoicism.

The choice of style helped the newspaper avoid charges, as the *Herald* had done previously, that the company had self-serving financial motives, or that the move was provoked by a desire to generate more income. The *Times* was aware of this potential criticism, and anticipated it in its own publicity by emphasizing, as the *World* had done, the serious responsibility of the newspaper to make a positive contribution in all matters of taste and culture:

> The *Times* does not deny that its building is commercial—utile dulci. That point must, in the nature of things and of buildings, particularly of buildings on the precious soil of Manhattan Island, be conceded as well as won. Yet as the possessor of a site so notable and conspicuous in a neighborhood rapidly undergoing architectural transformation, the *Times* did not feel at liberty to limit its ambition and its expenditure to a structure sufficing merely in the physical sense of its needs. It freely acknowledged and has respected its obligation to erect here a building which any city would deem an enhancement of its architectural distinction, and upon which no passer-by could gaze without pleasure.[47]

To this end, the *Times* erected a structure that was twenty-five stories and 362 feet high. The *Times* claimed that its building was the "city's tallest structure from base to top," although this was only true when measured in feet above sea level and when the underground stories were included. There were, in fact, buildings that were taller downtown, but because the Times Building stood in relative isolation uptown, these pronouncements went unchallenged. The building's central location also helped the newspaper assert its position "in the middle" and "at the heart" of the city's important activities. According to a radial picture of the building, the Times Tower stood at "the geographical centre of Manhattan: Battery four miles south, 125th Street four miles north, East river one mile east, North river one mile west,"[48] making it possible to overcome all of the traditional arguments about the importance of the Park Row location.

The detailed Building Supplement the *Times* published on January 1, 1905, also included a chart comparing the height of the other tall buildings in Manhattan, using measures such as "total floor space" and "cubical contents" to rank the *Times* first. Although not actually the tallest building in the city, it was able to make other true claims about its interior space as a result of a unique underground plan. Beneath the streets on all four sides, the building extended out well beyond the above-ground walls in a gigantic cavernous space housing the presses and the paper supply on three stories below ground. Above this, in the first subbasement, was rentable area and the mail delivery department; one story above this was the subway level, arcades, and the city delivery department. The subway station had been built as part of the very foundation of the Times Building, allowing employees to go directly from offices to the platform, and facilitating the distribution of the newspaper by allowing papers to go directly from the press to subway cars.[49]

Like several earlier newspaper buildings, the Times Tower had a well-known Italian structure as its influence. The building was based on the Campanile of Giotto in Florence, with the standard block-and-tower form adapted to fit the unusual dimensions of the Longacre Square site. The tower appeared to be a square, arising out of a rectangular block (although none of the four sides of the structure was even), and the footprint was actually wedge-shaped. The Gothic reinterpretation of the Florentine campanile helped to disguise these irregularities by adding three thick lower stories made of granite, with nine relatively unadorned stories above, capped with a richly ornamented capital with deeply inset three-story arcades. On top of this at the north end was a heavily sculptured tower with another thicker capital at the top of the tower. The building's exterior articulated its interior arrangement and also the hierarchy of offices, with the *Times* occupying the most ornate stories in the tower, and the lower, plain stories of the block housing offices for rent. The façade was made of "cream-white brick and terracotta," which, according to the Building Supplement, had "all the effectiveness of white marble, and add[ed] a singular charm of color."[50] The alleged superior height, the unique advantages of the location, and the Gothic styling all combined to produce what was, in the *Times's* estimation, the most perfect newspaper building that had ever been constructed. In their own reporting, the *Times* argued that newspapers had a special obligation to build in a striking fashion, because "a higher interest pertains, no doubt, to a newspaper building than to buildings as to which the public feels that it has less concern about what goes on within. The double appeal of the Times Building is marked and audible. It has deeply interested the community by its architecture and its situation. It now engages their attention as the home of this newspaper, equipped with every modern appliance, where matter written and put in type twenty stories or more above ground is printed upon presses fifty five feet below the surface of the earth."[51]

The Times Tower incorporated many common features of previous newspaper buildings, despite being built away from the traditional location. Over the half century of newspapers building on Park Row a notable uniformity to the discourse of these structures developed, largely because the newspapers established themselves as champions of their own interpretation. The use of superlatives, particularly surrounding height, was universal, even when not warranted. The internal layout of the buildings was also standard, with the presses in the basement, the public offices on the main floor, and the editorial and composition offices at the top. Much of this was functional. It made sense that the heavy industrial presses would be on the basement level where the floors were the most solid and light was not a requirement. For public convenience it was logical to place the subscription and business offices on the main floor giving them the most direct access to the street, and it was sensible to use the best natural light and air sources at the top for the composition and editorial rooms. But the symbolic aspect of these placements should not be overlooked. The publishers' offices were typically located on the highest level, with Whitelaw Reid's and Joseph Pulitzer's being the most extreme examples. As Frank Moss wrote of Park Row's response to the Tribune Tower, "Many were the envious cuts at the editor of the *Tribune* by those less fortunate editors who could not compose their editorials on such a lofty plane."[52] Pulitzer would surely not have been dismayed by the sightseer on the opening day of the World Building mistaking his office for God's.

The Times Tower in Times Square may have been the *New York Times* in stone, but it was a singularly ineffective newspaper building. It was almost immediately too small, it was difficult for trucks to access, and its narrow floors made putting together a large newspaper difficult. By 1913 the company moved most of its work to the Annex on 43rd Street, which ended up being renovated and enlarged four times. If newspaper buildings are any indication, the move to a larger structure was presented to the public as an outward sign of the company's stability and healthy growth, even if the company occupied no more space in the new building than it did in the old. The new building's

Park Row, 1936. (Photography Collection, Miriam and Ira D. Wallach Division of Art, Prints and Photographs, The New York Public Library, Astor, Lenox and Tilden Foundations)

value was not to be found in the larger interior space, but rather in the currency that the new exterior had for public relations. We know this because new buildings were often planned against the better judgment of shareholders, but representations of the new structure would adorn stationery, posters, postcards, envelopes, and any other surface that could be branded. As Elmer Davis wrote of the Tower in his history of the *Times*, "As an advertisement it is believed that the Times Building has been worth every cent it cost, and more, besides the reward that comes from the consciousness that its erection, in that place and at that time, was a public service."[53]

A new building also often coincided with other tangible changes at the newspaper, including the addition of new sections and less cluttered typography. These simultaneous measures demonstrate the synchronicity between the internal form and function of the newspaper and the external form and function of its architecture. Newspapers were becoming more accessible and more readable just as their buildings were helping to make urban space more

New York Times Annex, 229 West 43rd Street. (Picture Collection, The New York Public Library, Astor, Lenox and Tilden Foundations)

legible. Newspaper buildings had well-known European structures as their models, making their interpretation even more available to passersby, and when these classic styles did not supply their own explanation adequately, the paper issued page after page of appreciation and analysis to help the citizens of the city better understand them.

In the case of Times Square, the imprinting of the area in the public's consciousness went well beyond the striking figure of the tall and lean tower. What the *Herald* had done for the department store at 34th Street, the *Times* would do for the theater district and commercial culture of all kind. "The fact that the renaming of the square owed as much to the assiduous promotion of the new underground rail lines and the stunning real estate opportunities they opened as to the structure being celebrated, was quintessential New York style," wrote Ada Louise Huxtable.[54] So established is the name Times Square now that we rarely even link it to the newspaper from which it takes its name. But fusing the name of the paper into the landscape of the city was part of Adolph Ochs's deliberate plan; as David Dunlap would later write, "Talk about product placement."[55] The *Times*'s move to 42nd Street did more than move a newspaper headquarters. It reoriented the entire focus of news dissemination in the city. The crowds that once gathered in City Hall Park during major news announcements and celebrations, Ochs now brought to Times Square. He began by announcing the building with a fireworks display on New Year's Eve 1904, an instant tradition that was replaced by the dropping of the ball from the top of the tower the following year.

Newspaper owners like Ochs knew that their corporate identity was largely formed through the public's experience with the architecture of their company's headquarters, since people went to these sites in person to get the most recent news. In the pre-radio, -television and -Internet era, these buildings were especially important for determining people's relationship with media, and the crowds did more than signal the success of the paper: they were visible evidence of the paper's ability to convene a public.

The Times Tower at Times Square was the last of the major newspaper buildings to be constructed before 1922, when the *Chicago Tribune* erected its famous Gothic structure after a worldwide competition that established its architect Raymond Hood as a premiere architect of newspaper buildings. In 1930 Hood would be contracted to build the Art Deco showpiece on 42nd Street housing the *New York Daily News*. It may seem counterintuitive that in an era when radio was ascendant newspapers would continue to invest in grand architectural showpieces, but the print media industry retained a strongly held belief in the power of architecture to persuade. When all else is uncertain—the future of newspapers, the tastes of the public, economic stability, the threat of "new" media—the building is solid.

FOUR

# Art Deco News

This newspaper always will be fearless and independent. It will
have no entangling alliance with any class whatever—for class
feeling is always antagonistic to the interest of the whole people.
—Joseph Medill Patterson, June 26, 1919, from the
   *Daily News*'s first editorial and engraved on a wall of
   the building at 220 East 42nd Street

On April 9, 1921, a wake for the Herald Building at Broadway and 34th
Street featured Evelyn Scotney of the Metropolitan Opera Company singing
"Auld Lang Syne." The Stanford White structure, modeled after the Loggia of the Palazzo del Consiglio in Verona and one of the few exceptions
to the rule that media buildings rise as tall as the law and gravity allowed,
was now at risk of becoming an old acquaintance never brought to mind.[1]

Postcard of lobby and globe in the Daily News Building, ca. 1930.
(Author's collection)

The operatic farewell was a fitting tribute to the solemn event that marked the end of the august independence of the *New York Herald*. Following the death of James Gordon Bennett Jr. a year earlier, Frank Munsey, by then an inveterate newspaper consolidator, brought the *Herald* into the fold of papers that included the *New York Sun*, the *New York Press* and the *New York Evening Telegram*, signaling yet another episode in the ongoing crisis of the press.[2] The Reid family, owners of the *New-York Tribune*, would in short order purchase the *Herald* and merge it with their paper. The Rogers Peet Company, specializing in boy's and men's clothing, took over the Herald building for use as retail space, remodeling the inside but leaving the exterior intact, and the new company used the large street-level windows that once displayed the presses for the presentation of suits.

That the orderly and staid *Herald* had given way to a consumer showroom was a shift already embraced by the upstart *Daily News* across town, evidenced by the fact that in the same month Macy's finally relented and began advertising in the new tabloid.[3] Macy's had enjoyed a long and prosperous connection with the *Herald* across 34th Street, so this decision was a significant precursor of what was to come. Many of the more established businesses had kept their distance from the tabloids, fearing that their readers lacked the resources to shop or that having them in their stores might drive others away. The *News*'s own research department showed the folly of this thinking in their long-running campaign to "Tell It to Sweeney; The Stuyvesants Will Understand" that ran in *Editor & Publisher* and *Printer's Ink*.[4] "Sweeney" was the paper's shorthand for describing the ordinary city folk that other papers had largely ignored—discovered as the result of a remarkably thorough market research campaign in which Sinclair Dakin had found that the residents of New York's Lower East Side had greater margins of disposable income than many middle-class citizens and were avid consumers who embraced American brands as vehicles for assimilation. What looked to be insular immigrant communities from the outside turned out to be vibrant social networks eager to adopt the food, clothes, and habits of American life. As Dakin wrote, they wanted "grapefruit for breakfast, their own homes, a little car, money in the bank and a better future for the Sweeney juniors."[5] The *News* would cater to this new market with an approach that embraced the populist spirit better than any previous newspaper had, and was rewarded with the fierce loyalty of readers.

The paper was designed to attract and keep the attention of these readers by making them the subject of its news. The *News* provided crime, sports, and entertainment where the other papers focused on the market, finance, and politics. Its publisher, Joseph Medill Patterson, of the wealthy Chicago family that owned the *Chicago Tribune*, considered himself such an Everyman. Patterson, a former socialist, preferred the company of cab drivers to CEOs, was an avid filmgoer, and shunned vests and ties in the office.[6] In a publisher statement to the Audit Bureau of Circulation, the new tabloid was described as having been "modeled upon the lines of the highly successful illustrated dailies of London," specifically the *Daily Mirror*, which Patterson encountered during World War I. "Its aim is to give the day's news in pictures and condensed text. Its policy is to inform, instruct and amuse in a clean, wholesome fashion" and in so doing it was the first of many papers to see its mission as entertainment based, and not solely as an organ for news dissemination.[7] In the first issue of the *Daily News*, the opening paragraph of its editorial announced that "it will not be a competitor of other New York morning newspapers, for it will cover a field they do not attempt to cover."[8] This "field" was not a new terrain of news as much as it was a new group of readers, those not addressed by the existing broadsheets in the city. The editorial "Who We Are" self-consciously constructed the "we" as the public it aimed to serve, positioning the paper's writers and readers as one and the same.

The inclusivity of its first editorial continued in the paper's approach to illustration, where one central idea obtained: to show the news in photos rather than in words, or as Patterson repeatedly instructed his staff: "Think in terms of pictures."[9] The phrase to be used when describing the *News*, and its permanent modifying clause, was "New York's picture paper." Patterson coached his staff to "lay emphasis on romantic happenings and print pictures of girls who are concerned in romances, preferably New York girls. Also, one or more pictures every day with reference to a crime committed the previous day in New York. Please remember particularly, make it snappy, make it local, make it news."[10] Other staples of the paper included several features borrowed from the *Chicago Tribune*, such as "real love stories," "best jokes," "bright sayings of children," and "embarrassing moments" that could be used as needed. The paper offered money to readers supplying photos and stories, made a "daily pattern" available to home dressmakers to order, and presented a barrage of other circulation-building contests, games, and puzzles.

Such schemes served the obvious goal of driving reader interest and it was how the paper sought to speak to its readers directly: documenting their activities in the city and incorporating them in the everyday makeup of the paper. The *News* was to be nothing more and nothing less than a mirror of the city. By October of the first year it was clear to Patterson—who was still overseeing the paper from Chicago—that the paper's name was both unruly and redundant, and he recommended getting rid of it. He regretted having chosen "New York Illustrated Daily News," preferring instead "The Mirror" from the English tabloid. He suggested changing the name to the "News-Mirror" and then dropping the word "News," and must have been greatly annoyed when Hearst introduced the *New York Daily Mirror* in 1924.[11] Despite its name, however, the *Daily News* was designed most intentionally to function as a reflective surface, and readers were encouraged to see themselves in it. Patterson directed to his staff to put crowd pictures in every issue, taken at various locations including beaches, the Brooklyn Bridge, and Central Park, and to caption the photos with the query "Were You There?" The first ten readers to identify themselves in photos could present themselves to the *News* office to receive $5.[12] The mirror scheme was effective at populating the pages with the nonelite universe of readers and worked well in the era's edict of promoting surface over substance.

Informal polling on issues put the people's voice directly in the pages in their own words. Reporters were dispatched, for example, to "ask five girls if they smoke and then another day five young men if they object to their best girls or wives smoking."[13] Editorials provided a forum for debate on a range of issues from marriage to prohibition, and they were structured to give space to two well-known proponents on opposite sides of an issue in the hope of stirring up controversy while remaining somewhat neutral at the same time. One list of editorial ideas basked in the endless variety of opinions that could be solicited on a range of issues, from "the evils of the stage today—Dr. Straton to write one side, Gerry Farrar, Ina Claire, Elsie Ferguson, or some other woman star to write the other side" to "education vs. experience in fitting a man or woman for success in the business world" in which "Nick Murray Butler could take one side, Nathan Straus, or some other self-made man the other." A suggestion was made that "Anderson, the anti-saloon man, might tell us why America is better off under prohibition. Gov. Edwards could tell us why the country is not." For another, "Dr. Parkhurst, famous old vice investigator . . . on what he thinks New York needs most, Mayor Hylan could be tapped on the same subject."[14] Each issue took what the paper knew to be the central concerns of its readers to heart, liberally pitting young against old, male against female, and tradition against modernity, falling on no side more predictably than in a coin toss.

Other reader-friendly strategies included numerous contests that drew readers in, encouraged continued purchase, and gave out small sums of money in return for reader-generated content.[15] Most were beauty contests, which had the dual function of attracting both male and female readers and ensuring a constant supply of photographs of beautiful women; but sports, children, and humor figured prominently in others. A sampling of contests from the first two years included a

> $10,000 beauty contest, amateur photo contest, best jokes, embarrassing moments, bright sayings, real love stories, funniest motor experience, seeing New York photos, heroism awards, limericks, my burglary experience, strangest wedding I ever heard of, Dempsey-Carpentier contest, stingiest man, queerest boss I ever worked for, my nearest approach to death, title contest, funniest fish story I ever heard, soldiers' graves fund, mental telepathy, my best vacation experience, what the war has done for me, prize love story, swimming contest, Sally Joe Brown—friend in need, my experience with a woman hater, children to Coney Island, Venus contest, adoption of babies, shoes and stockings fund, funny face woman contest, beauty contest (Paramount); clothes for vest, toy party for children by Sally.[16]

Such contests pitted reader against reader in getting to the paper first, and eventually paper against paper in reaching prize-hungry contestants. In a circulation battle with Hearst's *American*, what began as an innocent lottery—in which readers collected coupons out of the paper, hoping they would match published numbers in later editions—escalated in a fury of one-upmanship between two publishers desperate to outdo the other. Hearst's Chicago paper, the *Herald and Examiner*, first offered $1,000 as a grand prize. The next day the *Daily News* announced a similar lottery with $2,500 to be won. Hearst went to $5,000 and the *News* went to $10,000; the *News* went to $15,000 and Hearst went to $20,000. Finally the *News* reported that it would go to $25,000, and should any other paper try to best them, they would double the purse. To keep the payouts from escalating any further, the *News* had Postmaster General Will Hays declare newspaper lotteries illegal.[17] And all of this took place before Hearst began his *Mirror*, which would seek to replicate every successful element of the *News* in a battle of tabloid against tabloid.

Important, too, were the aesthetics of the new paper. Not only was the *Daily News* smaller in size, its pages were clean and uncluttered. It discarded the traditional dense columns of text to accommodate enormous headlines and large, crisp, action photos. Its pages had energy inspired by the machine age, defying its two-dimensional form to convey constant motion. Photographers were forbidden to capture subjects looking directly into the camera's lens and were instructed to have them posing in the act of doing something. The old method of having men standing in a row and looking pleasant, it was said, was dead. As in the movies, people in pictures should not be standing still. According to Patterson, "Photos obviously posed and waited for are not so interesting."[18] Curlicues, border lines, and extraneous details were removed from the page for a more streamlined look.

These lessons were applied to the paper's offices as well. Already confident of the growth trajectory in 1919, Patterson asked his general manager William Field to prioritize their next steps: "A Sunday edition and an evening edition, a building of our own and admission in the New York City Press Bureau, and a first rate syndicate department."[19] Backed by the *Chicago Tribune*,

Daily News Building
at 23–25 Park Place.
(Getty Images)

the New York paper had the resources and access to capital that made all of these plans easily within reach. The paper began a photo syndicate, Pacific & Atlantic Photos, Inc., to guarantee access to news photos, and had use of the *Tribune*'s photo morgue as well. Circulation grew at an unprecedented rate, becoming the most-read morning paper in the country, with a daily circulation of 1 million in December 1925, and 1.2 million on Sundays.[20]

After a year of operation in the *Evening Mail* plant, the *News* took out twenty-one-year leases in modern loft spaces at 23–25 Park Place, and furnished it with high-speed presses for better picture printing.[21] When the Park Place space—still in close proximity to the other papers of Park Row—very quickly proved too small for the growing paper, Patterson looked to Midtown for his expansion, which had by the early twentieth century become a place where business, retail, entertainment, and newspapering was located. Acting as broker, the Douglas Elliman Real Estate Company amassed several parcels of land into an L-shaped plot that ran between 41st and 42nd Streets with a third frontage on Second Avenue. In putting together the large site several smaller plots had to be purchased and their tenants evicted, as was typical in building a large footprint in an already-developed area. Once the overall pattern of purchase became identifiable to existing landowners, of course, sale prices inevitably rose, and a rigorous set of negotiations ensued that saw demolition begin in some parts of buildings while tenants remained.[22]

The rectangle between 41st and 42nd would house the office tower portion of the building, and a nine-story arm jutting out to Second Avenue would hold the presses. As the structure was in the middle of a block rather than on a corner or plaza with a more advantageous approach, the challenge was to maintain some guarantee that the building would not be overshadowed by newer, taller buildings or lack sufficient light and air. To the east, this was achieved by the nine-story plant that would limit the height adjacent to the tower. To the west, an agreement was reached with the city Board of Education for the *News* to rebuild an existing school on the plot by sacrificing twenty-five feet of their own footprint in exchange for moving the school twenty-five feet farther west, producing a fifty-foot corridor between the News building and its neighbor. Thus, although only thirty-six stories high and placed in the middle of a block, the building had light, air, and views. The smaller floor plates would be worth, for the presence of windows on all four sides of the building, twice as much in rental income.

Despite his efforts to build a tower on a large site, Patterson resisted the notion that he was building a corporate headquarters, preferring instead to think of his new edifice as a factory. While this may have appeared as a nod to Patterson's working-class pretentions or to the fact that a majority of Americans now lived in cities and worked in factories rather than in agriculture, the insistence on this category of building type was also strategic in overcoming various zoning challenges encountered by the plan. In the dispute involving the building's classification (which would involve different building code regulations), the *News* argued forcefully on behalf of a "factory" designation. In a letter to the Board of Standards and Appeals, the company sought favor in the name of public interest. A different set of standards should apply, they claimed, given that the press, and the *News* specifically, was an amenity providing a public service:

> "THE NEWS" has the largest daily newspaper circulation in America. It disseminates news of current events to millions of New Yorkers. It is a quasi public institution required to keep the population in touch with news as or shortly after the happening of such current events. The press of the City renders to this extent a public service. The extent of such service to the public is, of course, measured largely by the facilities at the disposal of the corporation undertaking the publishing of the newspaper. The facilities for the publication of "THE NEWS" are at present inadequate. It will seriously prejudice its efficiency if is not permitted to enter into its proposed new building at the earliest possible moment.[23]

A compromise was found in having the building deemed "mixed occupancy," but the language used to describe the centrality of the paper's mission to the smooth functioning of the city was a strong indication of the advantageous position the media had when negotiating with the city. The careful straddling of both public and private interest demonstrates a canny flexibility in mobilizing either mission as the situation demanded.

## The News Building

These prosaic considerations aside, the News Building was of course designed to be much more than a factory for the production of a newspaper. As it had with credit, features, circulation, and advertising directors, the *News* once again borrowed from the *Chicago Tribune* in selecting Raymond Hood as its architect. Trained at the École des Beaux-Arts in Paris like many of his newspaper building predecessors, Hood was, with John Mead Howells, the celebrated architect of the 1925 Gothic Tribune Tower. For that prestigious and publicity-generating international architectural competition, in which some 263 architects submitted plans, Hood had not been invited to apply. It was his friend Howells who asked him to collaborate on a submission for the *Tribune* when he found out Hood was in need of work.[24] The *Tribune* competition, a twentieth-century public relations coup designed to celebrate the paper's seventy-fifth anniversary, offered $100,000 in prize money for winning submissions. As Katherine Solomonson has documented, the competition gave the paper an opportunity to "position itself as a cultural gatekeeper, affirming the editors' individual and institutional authority while advancing the interests of Chicago's business elite and, more broadly, of American capitalism." Publicity for the Tribune Tower appearing in the paper, according to Solomonson, aimed "to represent Tribune Company's corporate ideals through the most beautiful and distinctive office building in the world, and to produce a civic monument that would represent the values which an idealized, unified community would share with the Tribune. This monument would, in turn, set a new standard for commercial architecture, establish the superiority of American design, and contribute to Chicago's development into a city surpassing New York, or any other, in both beauty and economic clout."[25]

Where the Tribune Tower was clearly drawing on the advertising and publicity value recently accrued to the Gothic Woolworth Building in New York—"a giant signboard to advertise around the world"[26]—Hood's design for the *News* owed much more to the contemporary favor for streamlined, setback skyscraper design of the day than the classical paradigm he had trained in. The flying buttresses of the Tribune Building, so much remarked on for their Gothic elegance, were nowhere to be found at the News. Like the paper, the building was promoted on the basis of its newness; its break with older, outmoded ways of doing things; and as a standard against which all new buildings would be measured. Attaching itself to American ingenuity and the qualities seen as inherent in skyscraper design, the *News* advertised, "It is the latest and most perfect expression of the only new thing in architecture since the eighteenth century—the skyscraper, creature of the American mind and the American spirit. Built to house present-day business, the News Building has abandoned every classic canon, every mediaeval mannerism and ancient formula of architecture, and made its own. It copies nothing, repeats nothing. It is bare of battlements, arches, pillars, cornices, cupolas. It has no grinning gargoyles, no gilt grotesqueries, no obsolete ornament."[27]

Central to the modern design was its lack of crown. Instead of a complicated cornice at the top of the tower, the roofline appeared to be sliced off with a knife rather than tapering or finishing with a fancy dome or other flourish.[28] As in the pages of the paper the design suggested that nothing extraneous had been added; it was an expression of pure form, nothing embellished and nothing false. In classical architectural design the cornice is the signature of the building; in modern corporate image-making it functions as the building's trademark.[29] Here, alternating stripes of light and dark—white brick broken up with vertical rows of rectangular windows whose dark spandrel panels were continued by the use of dark window shades on the inside—contributed to the building's verticality despite the use of an elongating crown. For some critics the stripes evoked those of the American flag,[30] for others, the building's exterior played on the old newspaper saw, "black and white and read all over."[31] In design the thickness achieved by the flat roof was the same sleight of hand of the tabloid format compared to the traditional broadsheet: it made the form seem bigger than it was. It was undeniably tall, sleek, and streamlined—the very embodiment of Metropolis, via Fritz Lang, and fittingly gained fame as Clark Kent's workplace. Emerging as one of the fathers of Art Deco skyscrapers in the city, Hood's collection of buildings in Midtown—the McGraw Hill Building east on 42nd Street, the black-and-gold American Radiator Company Building south of Bryant Park, and the RCA Building at Rockefeller Center—remade the skyline using a new vocabulary of modernism as the epitome of corporate prowess.

The Zoning Resolution of 1916 enacted by the State Legislature was also central to the design of the building. The law, which became known as the setback law, promoted the wedding cake-profiles of many of the era's tall buildings, and dictated that a building's shape be determined by the width of the street it was on. The goal was to prevent the stifling lack of air and light that resulted from buildings that extended fully to their property line and continued straight up to the top, creating canyons of darkness in some of the more congested parts of downtown. The 1915 Equitable Building in lower Manhattan, at forty-two stories, was seen as one of the more egregious examples of mass-blocked skyscrapers; the 1916 law was set in place partly to prevent such buildings from being erected in the future. The new law stipulated that a building's tower could be infinitely high provided it only occupied 25 percent of the total building footprint, with the height of the first setback determined by an angle measured from the center of the facing street. It was in many respects a law that reached a sensible compromise between developers' desire for unchecked growth, and the needs of a population wanting light and air; and fortuitously, it garnered higher property values and rental incomes precisely as a result of these amenities.

Both Hood and Patterson knew that as profitable as the newspaper was—and it was extremely profitable—the building could only be sustainable with rental income, which, as Hood wrote in *Architecture Forum* in 1930, "is what makes it possible for *The News* to have its plant on an expensive, centrally located piece of property. This is a very valuable consideration for the newspaper, from all points of view,—collection of news, manufacturing and quick distribution of papers; but it would not have been a sound financial scheme but for the great revenue-producing office building."[32] The expense was justified on these grounds, and for the publicity such signature buildings were bringing to their corporate builders. Since the 1913 fifty-seven-story Woolworth Building at Broadway and Barclay opened in lower Manhattan, a new era of architecture as spectacle had emerged. The tallest building in the city at the time, Cass Gilbert's modern Beaux Arts Gothic tower directly across City Hall Park from Newspaper Row, opened to a flourish of media attention. Using coordinated press releases and a spectacular nighttime light show that drew attention from all directions, the Woolworth used the space before it in much the same way that the newspapers had: as a staging area for the spectacle of the building. The lesson of the Woolworth, the "Cathedral of Commerce" and a building guided by the logic of street theater, spectacle, and consumption, was not lost on the *Daily News*, then located behind it on Park Place.

The new era of media buildings in the 1920s, and most especially on 42nd Street, however, would make the Woolworth's Gothic seem an anachronism. Along the 42nd Street corridor, in the Grand Central Zone, Midtown began to rival the financial district in height, significantly altering the postwar skyline of New York. The Chrysler Building across 42nd Street helped establish the new order of corporate image-making in its self-conscious use of automotive decoration, making it a literal embodiment of machine-age styling. Setbacks were designated with gargoyles that recalled the hood ornaments of the Plymouth, while metallic hubcap-detailing circled the exterior. Noted for its seven-story stainless steel sunburst crown, the building was dedicated to "world commerce and industry" in a gesture familiar to those in the media industry making broad claims about the contribution their buildings made to elevating civilization and strengthening the character of their surroundings.

Though the *News* was farther east than any other paper, the location was meaningful to Patterson, who admitted that "I know I run a 'dirty rotten yellow sheet,' but if I can be on a crosstown street to Times Square I'll get my tabloids on the sidewalks in the morning ahead of any of my competitors."[33] The building was in many ways a monument to the readers of the yellow sheet, most tellingly in the frieze above the grand entrance on which the words (attributed to Abraham Lincoln) "He made so many of them" were etched. Depending on one's interpretation the phrase follows either "God must have loved the common people" or "common-looking people," or other, less generous salvos. The paper's intention was to speak directly to "the people," loosely defined, and the frieze rendered them in all their humble glory: pictured in hardhats, top hats, and bowlers; bearded and clean-shaven; in topcoats and in overalls; the men hold prospecting gear, shovels, toolboxes, and a newspaper. Women hold pocketbooks; one holds an

Frieze on the front of the Daily News Building, René Paul Chambellan. (Author's collection)

infant, while another holds the paw of a dog. Some walk in opposite directions as on a busy sidewalk while others crouch down against a backdrop of tall towers whose verticality echoes that of the News Building itself; it is a tableau *of* the front of the building *on* the front of the building.

The frieze's designer, René Paul Chambellan, an American sculptor trained at the École des Beaux-Arts, also designed the sculptures on the exterior of the Chicago Tribune Tower, the Radiator Building, and various pieces at Rockefeller Center. On the News Building façade were key elements of the new advertising milieu of the building. The sunrays, stylized in block form reaching out to a squared border, were echoed in the layout of many of the era's print ads. As Roland Marchand noted, the sunbeam was one of the visual clichés that implied an endorsement by God: "The subtly evocative power of the beam of light stemmed from the fact that it had become a secularized image without entirely losing its spiritual overtones."[34] The *New York Sun*, of course, used the ray motif in its paper's flag, but so did Crisco, Oldsmobile, and Kelvinator in advertisements of the period. The entire crown of the Chrysler Building was a crenellated sunburst. The logo of the Scripps Howard Company was of a lighthouse, whose beams of light shone in two directions. Appropriating all of the connotations of light and shine, as well as in this case reach, the graphic extension of "glow" served the same purpose that the *New-York Tribune*'s earlier clock tower and Pulitzer's gold dome had: it was a physical demonstration of dominion. Although the tower of the News Building was significantly stockier than earlier block-and-tower forms, the design's vertical lines nevertheless drew the eye to the top, and without lighting or expansive approaches to embellish its height, the sun rays work to suggest the same claim over the surrounding space that was to come under the paper's purview. The radiant beams were a constant in Art Deco design that along with chevrons and zigzag patterns conferred modernity as quickly and easily as the image of the skyscraper itself. But unlike these purely graphical and abstract forms, the sunburst played effectively on a natural phenomenon, albeit one that became denaturalized through the graphic precision of straight, sharp lines. The sun here, woven through the rounded edges of clouds, signifies more than shine and enlightenment, it suggests predictability and regularity, the cyclical nature of each day following into the next, the certainty that just as the sun will rise tomorrow, so too will there be a new edition of the paper. The rectangular frame of the frieze contains, in this way, daily life, just as the rectangular page of the *Daily News* contained each day.

Whether the frieze is a celebration of the common man or an indict-ment remains open to speculation. Patterson was not the first publisher in New York to celebrate (or take advantage of) the mass of readers with news and features designed to pander to their baser desires, and certainly not the first to enjoy a comparably better lifestyle; Pulitzer and Hearst had similarly populist approaches. Safely ensconced in penthouse suites, country clubs, private airplanes, yachts, or steamer cabins, most publishers would never be mistaken for one of their own readers. Their buildings elevated while their papers and their views often did not. Even Patterson, renowned as a man of the people, occasionally had somewhat derisive things to say about his readers; on the surprising popularity of crosswords in the paper he wrote. "I thought they would be too hard for the average slumster that inhabits New York."[35]

The subjects of the frieze—the people, light, and the quotidian—were also present in advertising for the building. Aware of the competition and glut of office space being built concurrently in the Grand Central Zone as a result of the fifty-six-story Chanin Building, the fifty-three-story Lincoln Building, and the soon to be completed seventy-seven-story Chrysler Build-ing across the street,[36] the campaign to sell the News Building to tenants emphasized light, proximity to Grand Central Station, and the building's distinctive style. The tower promised "the utmost in perpetual LIGHT and sunshine." No desk would be more than twenty-six feet from a window, and all modern amenities were provided. Sales entreaties offered "Offices of the future—today!" But as potential renters had only sketches to rely on, advertising had to go beyond a simple inventory of the building's features: "Preliminary to the actual construction of the building itself we have sim-ply an idea and a future to sell," wrote the publicity manager. The idea, as expressed in one ad, was "Glamour."

The image uses the straight diagonal lines of the sunbeam to cut across various walks of life, a cross section of actual and potential readers. Combin-ing glamour and entertainment—specifically the kind of entertainment that was a mainstay of the early 1930s cinema filled with class division and the promise of upward mobility—the visual tableau slices through the mundane and the heroic, while the text provides insight into the imagined reader with the familiar "we" of the paper's first editorial:

We enrich our own little limited lives with the versatility of events; thrill with emotions we shall never know, feast of fortune we shall never have,

Advertisement for the *Daily News*, printed in the *New York Times*, July 9, 1929.

enjoy second-hand shudders from crimes we shall never commit, quiver with courage that shall never be ours. Cinderella is not dead but rides in the subway each morning, with Carmen beside her. Launcelot [*sic*] languishes behind his spectacles, and earthbound Lindberghs are on every street, and that little man who wraps packages behind a counter is a miniature Morgan who never found Wall Street.

Out of this appetite for vicarious experience is born the innate craving for news, the fierce wish to know what others are doing, and thinking and feeling. Out of this human need has come the newspaper. And the audience and influence of any newspaper is occasioned not by its ministry to the mind, but by its salving of the spirit. . . .

It does not stress sensation, but in the calendar of contingencies called "news," it strives to convey some suspicion of the drama ceaselessly conducted in a world of conflict, some reflection of the romance of reality, some gauge of glamour that makes the present more palatable, the future more feasible.[37]

Providing pleasure and escapism during difficult political and economic times, and seeking progress through new technology, the *News* was doing on paper what the building's Art Deco style was doing on 42nd Street: it positioned the paper as a natural development that answered "the innate craving for news" and sidestepped the mind-body distinction in high- and low-brow news in favor of one that catered to the "spirit."

Such was the middle ground occupied by the paper's new headquarters. Despite the popularity of the style, then and now, Deco was not universally admired in the 1920s and '30s, particularly by fellow modernists. The conservative view held that socially turbulent times called for a strict allegiance to the comforting classical styles of the past, favoring Gothic spires and Beaux Arts symmetry. The more radical approach was to shed the shackles of the past to create newer, freer forms that were viewed as pure expressions of form without embellishment or artifice, as the Bauhaus school and the International Style advocated. The style that came to be called in the late 1960s "Art Deco," following from the *Exposition Internationale des arts décoratifs et industriels modernes* in Paris in 1925, had neither virtue. Deco was an inherently commercial style, associated with ocean liners, trains, and automobiles; dominated by chrome and silver; and, to purists, false materials that concealed true form. It was viewed as overly geometric and mechanical, taking inspiration from the factory cogs of the machine age, Mayan temples, and from the 1922 discovery of King Tutankhamun's tomb. Many of its most notable adopters, including Raymond Hood and the Chrysler Building's William Van Alen, were trained in the Beaux Arts tradition, leading critics to see their work as little more than stripped-down classicism. For practitioners Deco was cosmopolitan and urbane, while for others like Alfred Barr of the Museum of Modern Art, it was "the taste of real estate speculators, rental agents and mortgage brokers."[38] In its alignment with the middlebrow, Deco had neither the authenticity of the vernacular nor the high-art aspirations of the International Style. It was complicit with consumer capitalism in a manner that earlier papers, and contemporaneous buildings to the east like the Times Building, sought emphatically to deny through recourse to designs more evocative of cathedrals than corporate offices. Such mass appeal, however, was precisely in keeping with the goals of the *News*, and it openly celebrated the commercialism of both its paper and its headquarters.

Where nineteenth-century news buildings had placed their allegorical features on the outside, the News Building with its lobby globe drew the public inward. The globe, still present in the lobby of the building despite the departure of the *News* to 33rd Street and Tenth Avenue in 1985, signals

Daily News Building at 220 East 42nd Street, Raymond Hood, 1930.
(Photography Collection, Miriam and Ira D. Wallach Division of Art,
Prints and Photographs, The New York Public Library, Astor, Lenox and
Tilden Foundations)

another of the through-lines in media architecture. Representing the Renaissance aspiration for comprehensiveness in human knowledge, globes
have figured prominently in museums and in the private studies of the
wealthy as emblems of worldliness. Just as the fashion for miniaturized globes
that could be worn on a watch chain showed a cosmopolitan outlook for
nineteenth-century gentlemen, the globe in the lobby is a public statement
of the breadth of the newspaper upstairs. As a promotional brochure boasted,

"For the home of a publication devoted to the news of the world the lobby of the News Building is especially appropriate."[39] The globe, said to be the largest in the world at the time of construction, and the centerpiece of the $200,000 lobby, weighs 4,000 pounds, inclined at 23.5 degrees, oriented to true north, and makes a full revolution every ten minutes. On the floor, radiating out from the sunken globe, is a giant compass pointing to fifty-eight world cities and showing their distance from New York. The walls are adorned with seventeen panels of charts and instruments illustrating the movement of the earth, a moonlight chart, maps, time zones, weather, wind velocity, atmospheric pressure, and other assorted metrological equipment. To this, Joseph Medill Patterson is reported to have countered: "Weather charts! What people want are 'murder charts': some kind of map of the metropolitan area where the latest crimes could be chalked up."[40] Yet the striking showpiece lobby was of great value in wooing tenants to the building and it was circulated widely in postcard form.[41]

In a mutually reinforcing dynamic, the building lent new prestige to the *News*, both internally and to its peers. As Leo McGivena wrote, "It was substantial evidence of its success and prosperity, commanded the respect and admiration of the business community."[42] And for some observers, the building governed the news being written on the inside: "Its content of non-erotic news has greatly increased since 1930. . . . It just doesn't seem right, they say, to be baldly indelicate in such a monumental structure as the Daily News Building."[43]

If there was a change in the comportment of newsmakers toward greater restraint, there was also a reorientation to the changing media landscape of the 1930s that echoed the new rhythms of radio, cinema, typography, and advertising. Helping to capture the increased pace of movement, speech, and daily occurrences, Mark Hellinger wrote a Broadway gossip column in the Tommy-gun style of Walter Winchell and Damon Runyon. Like many of the news writers of the day who landed in Hollywood, he based his stories on Broadway characters in films like *Broadway Bill* (1934), *The Roaring Twenties* (1939), *It All Came True* (1940), and *The Killers* (1946), and most memorably as the direct address narrator in *The Naked City* (1948). Patterson—an avid filmgoer who had a handful of favorite screen actresses on whom he lavished generous space in his paper—promoted the drama and motives of characters in film as a style of writing: "The News is more than a record of fact and incident. It is a daily cinema of the news stream. It interprets elementary interests instead of rendering routine reports. It cares little for important names or formal events. It seeks the story behind the story. It believes that motive is more interesting than murder, consequences more important than commission, that what people think and feel is more significant than what they do."[44] In this spirit, the paper also began a course on scenario writing by Anita Loos and John Emerson, serialized in the *News* in daily installments.[45] Taking cinema as a stylistic cue was only one of the ways that the *News* and its building were both reflecting and constructing the new media landscape of the 1930s. Both were attentive to motion and speed, current with the appetites and desires of their readers.

Although the *News* did not start its own broadcasting arm until it built WPIX as a television station, Patterson had been long intrigued by the power of radio and corresponded with many other newspapers to solicit their opinions on whether starting a radio station was good practice for newspapers.[46] The Tribune Company had of course pioneered the development of radio with its own station in Chicago, WGN—its name (World's Greatest Newspaper) undeniable evidence of the power of the new medium to help publicize newspapers. The lobby of the News Building suggests that in many ways this was a radio building as much as it was a newspaper building, sharing more in common with Hood's design for the RCA Building and Radio City at Rockefeller Center than with previous newspaper edifices. Both Patterson and Hood easily embraced the architecture-as-media/media-as-architecture conflation that did not draw a distinction between what the paper could do every day and what the building could do over the long term. By using entertainment as a vehicle through which news could be delivered, no clear distinction was made between informing, educating, uplifting, or amusing the public in architecture or in putting out a daily paper.

That architecture would play a role in the advertising strategy of media companies—as in other industries—had already been established, but never before the News Building had it been so openly celebrated. The public relations value of the building was its primary value, as noted by contemporary observers: "Hood's theory, as a strict utilitarian, is that a skyscraper can properly be made to advertise the company which owns it."[47] Writing in *The Nation*, Douglas Haskell called the Daily News Building "architecture as advertising art."[48] S. J. Wolff in the *New York Times Magazine* concluded of Hood that "Traditions . . . mean nothing to him except as hurdles which must be jumped in order to keep pace with the fast tempo of modern life. In the New York buildings which were born on his drafting table he has disregarded old ideas: columns and capitals have been swept away and pilasters have given place to windows; splotches of color have given variety to unbroken surfaces. He has reared no temples to dead gods; he has built workshops for living men and in their construction he has proclaimed the era of business, of machinery and speed."[49]

Arthur Tappan North, too, saw the new building as more than a newspaper factory. "The incorporation of publicity or advertising features in a building," he wrote, "is consonant with and is a legitimate attribute of good architecture. It stimulates public interest and admiration, is accepted as a genuine contribution to architecture, enhances the value of the property and is profitable to the owner in the same manner as are other forms of legitimate advertising."[50] As soon as it was completed the image of the Daily News Building adorned all business correspondence, further solidifying the building-as-advertisement concept like so many newspapers had done before. By then, as Robert Biggert has shown, the practice of having a rendering of one's headquarters on company stationery had become common practice: hotels, retail outlets, clubs, and other businesses serving the public carried flattering images of their structures on all manner of printed material. And for those corporations after the turn of the century that had been accused of "soullessness," renderings of factories and downtown headquarters gave form and identity to large, faceless entities, just as images of founders, presidents, and their signatures adorned trade cards and advertisements.[51]

The signature skyscraper on 42nd Street housing the *Daily News* was notable for its celebrity architect, its location, and that it was home to the city's fastest growing tabloid. It was a showpiece that amused and entertained, impressed corporate tenants, and drew so much public interest to the lobby that a second entrance had to be built for employees. But it was not the only Deco news structure of the era, and it was not the first. Hearst's *Daily Mirror*, which adopted every successful strategy of the *News* in an effort to beat it at its own game, had erected a loft style Deco building a year earlier at 235 East 45th Street, designed by the prolific Manhattan architect Emery Roth. This building, which continues to house Hearst operations including offices for A&E, the History Channel, and *Biography* magazine, got significantly less notice in the architectural and general press of the day, likely because it got lost amidst the flurry of real estate news that Hearst was then generating. Of the few renderings in the architectural press, one exists purely to advertise the new offices of *American Architect*, a tenant. Completed in 1928, the sixteen-story building was located perilously close to the abattoirs along First Avenue, and despite having been designed by Roth (who erected

Daily Mirror Building, 235 East 45th Street, Emery Roth, 1928. (*The American Architect*, 1929)

more glamorous apartment buildings and hotels in the city than any other architect of his era), it was considered a rather workaday building. Hearst and Roth were responsible for so much development in Manhattan at the time that this building did not merit much attention, but it did adhere to the new direction being taken by media edifices in the 1920s. Built in Midtown in the Deco style, as was Hearst's South Street plant in lower Manhattan that housed the *Journal American,* it was sometimes known as the "Grand Central Advertisers Building" owing to the number of tenants in the industry. The two entrances flanking the Daily Mirror building are also adorned with radiant sunbeams as at the News Building.[52]

The *New-York Tribune,* when still controlled by Whitelaw Reid and his wife Elizabeth, with their son Ogden as president, had moved from Park Row to 40th Street in 1923. Theirs was a less publicized construction project that did not seek aggrandizement in architecture as much as in location, but it may have signaled more about the future than some of the other showpieces. The new Tribune Building was lauded for its size, doubling its space to 100,000 square feet, and capable of accommodating the growing staff and the paper's

Display ad, *New-York Tribune,* April 28, 1922, and April 17, 1923.

presses. Finding that "it frequently becomes necessary to omit large quantities of advertising, which could find place only by the sacrifice of news," the *Tribune*'s move to Midtown was presented as necessary to meet the "unprecedented increase in circulation and business." The *Tribune*'s new building was in form what Patterson claimed his building to be but wasn't: it was a factory. The edifice took up a 15,000-square-foot plot and rose only seven stories, but all were occupied by the paper's operations with no extraneous rental space.

The *Tribune*'s claims on the publicity value of the building were pointedly denied, paradoxically, in advertising. One ad asserted that the building "is not intended as a monument or advertisement," while another more directly invoked the Daily News Building: "The new plant was not planned as an industrial shrine to attract the casual visitor to New York."[53] Instead, the building was said to have been "planned solely in an earnest effort to provide a model modern newspaper publishing plant."[54] Modern, here, was an appeal not to surface aesthetics but to efficiency and science, and streamlining was not an external style template but a description of the increased speed with which the new plant could produce news. "Gravity" was the keyword in the new organization, by which was meant not seriousness, but rather a literal gravity that governed the movement of newspaper operations from the top of the building to the bottom. Thus copy would travel from the upper floors down through editorial, composing, and stereotyping, to the pressroom and onto delivery trucks. "News," in this scheme, as at all other news buildings up to this point, physically traveled through the building as it written, edited, and set. Echoing the Fordist logic of the automobile plant,[55] information is the metal that gets hammered and molded on its way to becoming a newspaper. The building must make allowances for the movement of copy and the people and machines that carry it from place to place. After computers automated newsrooms, this model of interior architecture would cease to exist.[56]

With little pretense to corporate symbolism, the Tribune Building's main façade was composed of bays for delivery trucks. Foremost among the reasons for the move, however, was its uptown location: "Until recent years the great body of morning newspaper readers could be served by a delivery system which made situation of the plant unimportant. But the city is rapidly moving into the country, and the morning newspaper must follow population. Suburban circulation has become so great that a plant well situated with reference to railroad terminals is essential to a successful morning newspaper."[57] In the paper's editorial on the day of the move, Park

Row is cast into the past: "With the Tribune's move to West Fortieth Street, Printing House Square becomes a memory. Here was the natural newspaper center for the New York that has now receded into the distance."[58]

Despite the prominence of these newer buildings in Midtown, two news organizations maintained their lower Manhattan presence in defiance of the belief that papers follow the population. Horace Trumbauer's building for the *New-York Evening Post*, at 75 West Street, was a Deco building that took advantage of its proximity to the Hudson River for newsprint delivery. Here again the 1930 News building overshadows the public record of this earlier venture. By the 1920s the *Evening Post* was already one of the longest surviving papers in the country, having been founded by Alexander Hamilton in 1801 and stewarded through the nineteenth century by William Cullen Bryant; in 1897 it passed from Henry Villard to his son Oswald Garrison Villard. However, ownership transferred several times after the turn of the twentieth century. In the 1920s, the *Evening Post* was owned briefly by Cyrus Curtis, then a formidable media entrepreneur responsible for the *Saturday Evening Post*, the *Country Gentleman*, and the *Ladies Home Journal*. The Curtis Publishing Company had limited interest in newspapers, but the Philadelphia-based empire owned the *Public Ledger* and *The Inquirer* in that city, and from 1923 to 1934, the *Post* in New York. Trumbauer was a Philadelphia architect who gained fame as a builder of country homes for the very wealthy and a great many large projects in Philadelphia including hospitals, hotels, and the Art Museum. As the architect of Duke University and Harvard's Widener Library, he was well known among the elite, although with a smaller portfolio in New York. He built the Duke townhouse on the Upper East Side, and had worked on the annex to the World Building on Park Row, and as the designer of the Public Ledger Building in Philadelphia he was Curtis's choice to build the home of the *Post* in New York.

The *Evening Post* had previously occupied a nearby building at 20 Vesey Street (designed in 1906 by Robert Kohn), a landmarked Art Nouveau structure that attempted to capture on its exterior the history of journalism in its ode to bygone printers on its spandrels and statues to the "Four Periods of Publicity": the Spoken Word, the Written Word, the Printed Word, and the Newspaper. After twenty years at this building, the move to West Street was advertised on the basis of improved light and air, with the half-acre site allowing for expansion as needed. Where previous news buildings had boasted their proximity to the courts, police headquarters, and Western Union, the west side location was favored for its access to "transit lines, the

Evening Post Building, Horace
Trumbauer, 1926. (Museum of
the City of New York)

Stock Exchange and Curb Market and to the great commercial districts."[59]
Its presses occupied the first floors, with the newspaper offices above, and
rental floors above those. The structure is notable for its inventive use of
polychromatic terra cotta cladding on the upper floors, which combine with
the abrupt setbacks to evoke an ancient Mayan temple.

Like the News Building, the adherence to the 1916 zoning law resulted
in setbacks on all sides at floors seven, fourteen, and sixteen. Outfitted with
the latest in modern printing equipment and designed with a penthouse
apartment for the Curtis family to use when in New York, the investment
nevertheless did not survive past Curtis's death in 1933. The paper changed
hands several times before Dorothy Schiff acquired it and transformed it
into a tabloid.[60]

In February 1931, the Evening *World*, Morning *World* and Sunday *World*
were sold to the Scripps Howard Company and merged with the *New York
Evening Telegram*, a paper once held by the Bennetts of the *Herald* and sold
to Frank Munsey. After Munsey's death, the Scripps Howard chain acquired

*New York World-Telegram*,
Howell and Thomas.
(Cleveland Public Library Fine
Arts & Special Collections)

FOUR GREAT NEWSPAPERS . . . IN ONE!

Ad for the newly merged *New York World-Telegram* newspaper, *New York Times*,
March 2, 1931.

the *World* (against the wishes expressed in Joseph Pulitzer's will that his papers never be sold) because Herbert, Ralph, and Joseph Pulitzer Jr. could not continue to operate profitably. The formation of the *New York World-Telegram* occasioned the construction of a new home for the hybrid paper, and the employees of the *World* reluctantly moved from the gold-domed Park Row tower to a new ten-story, $3 million building facing West Street on the block between Barclay and Park Place, across the street from Ralph Walker's 1927 Deco New York Telephone Building, and a few blocks north of the New York Post building.

Although the paper resided in lower Manhattan, advertising for the merger reflected the Midtown orientation of its main competitors. The March 2, 1931 ad, "Four Great Newspapers in One," shows the paper floating over 42nd Street with a clearly visible Chrysler Building and Daily News Building at right. With its own noticeably workaday office building rather than an architectural showpiece, the advertising works to infuse the new paper with all of the symbolic spirituality seen in the Deco-style rays of light of its contemporary competitors' structures. Mimicking Michelangelo's *The Creation of Adam* fresco in the Sistine Chapel, the image consecrates the newly formed paper.

Despite the building boom ushered in during the Deco skyscraper period and the newspapers' transformation to the tabloid format, little in the way of construction would take place in the following years. New architecture in the media industry would slow considerably, but the location of news plants was soon to return to its former importance when delivery strikes brought suburban readers back downtown looking for their news.

# FIVE

# Postwar News

This merger represents for each of us a break with a long tradition.
It represents a new direction for our individual publishing interests
with all the attendant hardships.
—William Randolph Hearst Jr., Jack R. Howard, and
John Hay Whitney, "Text of Statement on Papers' Merger,"
*New York Times*, March 22, 1966

By 1945, New Yorkers were getting used to taking their papers with double-
barreled names—the *World-Telegram*, *Journal American*, and *Herald Tribune*—
but they were soon to have difficulty taking them at all. Unlike the two
more famous New York newspaper strikes of December 1958 and December
1962 to March 1963, the 1945 strike did not hit during the holiday season, a
blessing perhaps to advertisers, but no gift to families waiting to read about

Times Square postcard, ca. 1920. (Author's collection)

returning soldiers. The major papers—the *New York Times, New York Herald Tribune, New York World-Telegram, New York Journal American, Wall Street Journal, New York Sun, New York Post, Daily News, New York Daily Mirror,* and *Brooklyn Daily Eagle*—along with the *Brooklyn Citizen,* the Long Island *Daily Star-Journal* and *Bronx Home News,* all belonged to the Publishers Association of New York City and their deliverers to the News Mailers and Deliverers Union (NMDU), who put their deliverers in a strike position as of 12:01 A.M. Sunday, July 1, 1945. In anticipation of a strike many drivers failed to show up to work on Saturday, and knowing that the papers would likely not be delivered, the usually large Sunday print runs of these papers were cut back dramatically.[1] A simultaneous International Typographers Union strike in Jersey City and Bayonne, New Jersey, made the dearth of newspapers a regional, rather than simply a municipal, epidemic.

The summer of 1945 saw an estimated 425 strikes taking place in the United States. The *Chicago Tribune* reported that the high volume of activity was attributable to the war's end; that "victory in Europe, with its seed in union rivalry, unsettled grievances in war plants, and a reawakening struggle for local union leadership" made for unusually high levels of labor unrest.[2] Having won important concessions in some industries and not others, the increasingly powerful trade associations the American Federation of Labor (AFL) and the Congress of Industrial Organizations (CIO) sought to improve working conditions across a wide variety of industries. Newspaper plants, unlike many others, did not have to be retrofitted back to domestic production from munitions making, and the basic technology had changed little during the 1940s—but working conditions were similar to those in other production facilities: "heavy, dirty, physical work, requiring real muscle power and athletic limberness" as Richard Kluger wrote.[3] Newsprint rations, which took effect in 1943, may have lessened the load of each individual paper, but did nothing to lighten the burden for the deliverers. Bundles continued to roll off the presses, and the demand for war news kept readers and news dealers anxious for timely deliveries. The hours were long, and the pay was minimal. Vacations were unpaid, and there were no medical benefits nor retirement fund. Despite the production schedule that demanded around-the-clock work, the graveyard shift was not compensated any differently than the day shift. Newspapers were uniquely vulnerable to any form of work stoppage because news cannot be printed in advance in anticipation of a strike, and missed days can never be made up for later.

The 1945 strike caused major urban papers to scale back their advertising as a result of vastly diminished circulation. The *Herald Tribune* printed only items of public notice, including death notices, and the *Brooklyn Eagle* dropped all of its ads except at the insistence of advertisers.[4] The *New York Post* and the *Bronx Home News*, who shared owners, stopped publishing altogether on the second day of the strike.[5] Advertisers, including the newspapers themselves, began buying air time on local radio stations, for which the stations demanded premium rates. Those who turned to television, still an infant medium, did not venture far into the live-motion capabilities of moving pictures with sound; many simply held up the newspaper ads in front of the camera. On a screen a fraction of the size of a modern television screen, the visual impact was underwhelming. Most famously, Mayor Fiorello La Guardia read an installment of Dick Tracy out of the *Daily News* over his weekly radio address on WNYC. The first week of the strike he did it as a service to the "kiddies," the second week, after hearing from radio producers what an enjoyable *visual* performance he gave, newsreel cameras were there to capture his reading. On the streets, live models were hired to wear sandwich boards around high-traffic areas like Grand Central Station and in department store windows.

The damage wrought on the city's economy was manifold. Broadway shows closed in the absence of ads and reviews. Moviegoers could not consult show time listings in the paper so theaters were sparsely populated. Sports scores went unreported and stock market prices were a mystery. In every industry the lack of a daily newspaper was felt in myriad ways. Apartments went unrented, jobs went unfilled, and funerals unattended. Florists suffered for lack of funeral attendance. Without a newspaper to inform them, people were at a loss for conversation topics, entertainment guides, and necessary daily information.[6]

One of the legacies of this and subsequent newspaper strikes in New York was the expansion of news coverage on the radio. The *Times, Herald Tribune, Sun,* and others scheduled regular broadcasts of updates that people could tune in to listen to. What could have been a boon to radio, however, turned out to be, at least in the estimation of the newspaper industry, a missed opportunity. Columnists who wrote postmortems on the strike argued that listening to the news would always be inferior to reading it, that depth in news analysis could only be delivered in print, and that radio had not taken advantage of the position of privilege it found itself in. There was little surprise in this, since radio did not yet have its own news staff, and did little more than read the newspaper on the air. But the general feeling was that radio was a perfectly good medium for receiving weather and traffic reports, music, and entertainment news, but that it could never be taken seriously for anything else. This may have been a purposeful effort to contain the threat posed by the new media through trivialization, but in the era before newspapers became part of large broadcasting empires, such critiques of radio and television were commonplace.

With alternative platforms for news still seen as too limited, the *World-Telegram*, *Sun*, *Journal American*, *Herald Tribune*, and *Times* opted to sell limited editions of their papers directly from their plants,[7] putting news buildings back to their former place of prominence in readers' minds at a time when many could be forgiven for not knowing where the buildings were located. Five decades earlier, when most New York papers were congregated along Park Row in lower Manhattan, it was typical for readers to go physically to the newspaper offices between editions. They did so not only to place classified ads or renew their subscriptions (for which an in-person transaction was the most efficient), but also to get the news. Between editions, or during high-volume news events like elections, newspaper building façades carried the latest news while the buildings themselves functioned as billboards for their tenants (see chapter 2). In the 1920s newspaper buildings were able to bring people together even for events that occurred over radio, just so that people could be together to celebrate.[8] By midcentury the location of newspaper offices had become a matter of little consequence to many readers, and the buildings were more often referred to as "plants" or "factories" than architectural showpieces. The concentration around Printing House Square had dispersed, and the location of the news operation mattered much less to readers. Orders could be sent by telephone or by mail, and newspapers were delivered to the door or easily purchased at one of thousands of street-corner newsstands. People knew that Times Square was where the *Times* was, but they didn't have to go there in person except to celebrate New Year's Eve. The *Daily News* had its grand Art Deco palace at 42nd Street, but it too functioned as a place for tourists to visit rather than a space for the general public to receive their news. But in an era when the newspaper office was also its plant, the newspaper building was the source of the actual newspaper, and when strikes threatened circulation, the role of the building returned, briefly, to a place of preeminence, allowing these structures once again to fulfill their role as an advertising platform for their brand.

The papers reported and photographed their daily sales from plants as a new barometer of their popularity in place of official circulation rates.

*New York Journal American* during strike. (Getty Images)

Circulation inflation took the form of waiting for the line to be at its longest before photographing it for the paper the following day, as was the case at Hearst's *Daily Mirror.*[9]

That any line at all formed at the *Journal American* was surprising, given the building's location. The plant at 220 South Street on the East River would have been easily accessible to nineteenth-century Park Row denizens, but it was miles away from the new Midtown corridor of newspaper offices. So during the strike the paper hired shuttles to transport readers to the plant in an effort not to be left behind in the new competition for customers. The *Daily News* claimed a line of seventeen blocks long, and eager readers were advised to exit the subway at 34th Street rather than 42nd Street to be closer to the line's end.[10] The *Times* reported the arrival of "more than 60,000 persons a day to get their morning newspaper . . . by subway, auto and taxi, from all five boroughs and from points beyond in Long Island and New Jersey."[11] The activity at the building sites was of course generating news as well, as buyers clashed with strikers on picket lines. Single-issue purchasers were generally left alone, while those attempting to buy in bulk for later resale were swiftly approached by picketers, resulting in arrests at both the Daily News and the Times Buildings.

That architecture could again be used for the purpose of advertising newspapers, as strikes forced buildings to stand in for the absence of their product in the marketplace, was an unintended consequence of the labor dispute, and readers gathered at newspaper buildings much as they had in the nineteenth century. The *Daily News* produced a short promotional film, *Seventeen Days: A Story of Newspaper History in the Making*, chronicling the strike and showing the activity at each of the city's plants. The narrator berated New Yorkers for taking the complicated mechanisms of printing and delivery for granted: "Part of this normal life was newspapers, taken as a matter of course, by everyone. So regular and complete a part of normal everyday living that finding newspapers on the newsstands, buying them morning and night was taken pretty much for granted. Never a thought of the rumbling presses that produced them. Completely oblivious to the vast transportation system that placed them so conveniently on 14,000 strategically located newsstands throughout the city. No reason to contemplate what life without newspapers would mean. Until suddenly and with little warning: STRIKE!"[12]

The papers unaffected by the strike were those whose labor practices, in line with their editorial policies, had already reached favorable agreements with the deliverers. These included the *Daily Worker, Jewish Morning Journal*, and the *Jewish Daily Forward*.[13] The single "mainstream" newspaper not struck was *PM*, a small, five-year-old tabloid experiment run by Ralph Ingersoll and Marshall Field III, the department store heir. What made the paper experimental was also what kept it from being considered entirely mainstream. The paper was emphatically pro-labor, and its motto, "We're against people who push other people around," found numerous possible editorial crusades, against all manner of corporate bullying and government malfeasance. Most unusual was the paper's policy to accept no advertising. It was to survive on the cover price of ten cents alone. The paper's investors were a group of wealthy New York liberals invited by Ingersoll, formerly of the *New Yorker*. Those who willingly put up $150,000 as an initial contribution included magnate Jock Whitney, A&P supermarket heir Huntington Hartford III, book publisher Lincoln Shuster, and Elinor Gimbel and Marshall Field, of the eponymous department stores.[14] That such inveterate advertisers should want to publish a paper in which their own concerns could not buy space may have seemed counterintuitive, but the mandate of the paper was that in such politically charged times news be unfettered by corporate interests, and the only guarantee of truth was independence.

As a newspaper experiment, *PM* broke significant new ground. Its layout and design were striking, with images provided by the leading photographers of the century, including Margaret Bourke-White and Weegee (Arthur Fellig). Its distinctive burnt-orange accent on the front page made it graphically forceful, standing out against the gray tones of its rivals on the newsstand. Inside, writing by Dashiell Hammett, Ernest Hemingway, Dorothy Parker and Dawn Powell could be found. Dr. Seuss (Theodor Geisel) was the paper's first political cartoonist. It was first among New York papers to include radio and movie listings, and its photographic section "Picture News" continued as "Parade," a magazine insert found in newspapers across the country.[15] As a newspaper model, however, *PM* was not a resounding success: its lack of advertising made drastic cuts necessary, and by September of its first year of operation, Marshall Field had bought out the first investors at twenty cents on the dollar, leaving him as the sole owner.[16]

In 1944, in time for its fourth anniversary, *PM* moved from its original quarters in Brooklyn, where it used the presses of the *Brooklyn Daily Eagle*, to the basement and first four floors of 164 Duane Street.[17] Its unassuming 1911 building was twelve stories tall, had been designed as an office building by Rouse and Goldstone, and was situated in one of the few remaining manufacturing areas in the city.

*PM* was not outwardly thrilled to have the audience all to itself for the duration of the strike. The paper had already established its pro-labor stance, signaled by the fact that the deal they had made with their deliverers was already better than what the strikers were asking for. They did not appear to take any pleasure in holding the only title in a one-newspaper town, and even if they had, they did not have enough paper to fully exploit the situation: "We do not relish the position we are in of largely monopolizing the newsstands during this temporary period. We believe that the more newspapers there are serving the people, and the keener the competition, the more chance there is that the truth will be served."[18] *PM* quickly responded to the dearth of papers by choosing to reprint what it judged to be the most newsworthy items from other papers. Opting to take a nonadversarial role toward its competitors, it selected important stories from the other papers and reprinted them verbatim, giving readers a chance to see at a glance what the major stories were.

> Freedom of the press is pretty remote to the man who has no choice in the paper he must read, even, we admit, if the paper is PM. Most of the newspaper readers of this country, unfortunately, are in just that position, for in most but the largest cities—and in some of them, too—there is only one paper or one morning paper and one afternoon paper, sometimes under the same ownership. In such communities, the reader isn't even in a position to buy another paper as a yardstick, to find out if his own paper is giving him all the facts, lying to him, short-changing him, serving his interests or serving the interests of someone else. The next time you hear someone arguing against Government action to open up monopolized channels of news such as the AP, you might think about the implication of monopoly journalism to the man who buys a paper.[19]

With this new news almanac, *PM* was recreating the busy, cheek-by-jowl atmosphere of the earlier Park Row bulletin boards: allowing readers to view all papers at once and make choices according to their own taste.

Neither *PM* nor the sale of single-copy papers at newspaper plants would be enough to sustain the industry for the next two decades. New York papers were besieged by strikes, as were papers in most other American cities, including Detroit (which saw eight strikes in seven years), Cleveland, Minneapolis, St. Louis, Milwaukee, and others.[20] In New York these ongoing labor disputes were seen as the catalyst for the demise of many of the city's longest running papers. In 1953, a sixteen-day strike by photoengravers closed six papers for eleven days. A nineteen-day strike in 1958 hit nine papers, all of which continued to publish except for the *Daily News*, where printers refused to cross the deliverers' picket lines. Both of these strikes took place in December, when advertisers generally anticipate both a higher volume of ad buys and sales. The year 1962 saw strikes at twenty-four daily newspapers across the country, including the 114-day strike that began in December that closed the *Times, Daily News, World-Telegram,* and *Journal American.*[21] Out of solidarity the unions at the *Herald Tribune, Daily Mirror* and *Post* were also struck. The newspaperless city once again led to a return to nineteenth-century modes of communication. Sterns department store put young women in their store windows not to model clothes but to write advertising messages on chalk boards.[22] This time television, in addition to radio, stepped in to fill the void, increasing newscasts from fifteen minutes or less to thirty minutes.

## *Herald Tribune*

By 1957 the *Herald Tribune* was in desperate need of capital investment, and the multimillionaire John Hay (Jock) Whitney, American ambassador to England and a former investor in *PM*, was a supporter of the paper who did not want to see it close. In a report by one of his financial advisors, Whitney was given a candid assessment of the situation at the paper:

> The failure of the *Tribune* to build circulation and advertising volume during the past ten years, especially the dramatic decline in its share of Sunday circulation and advertising lineage, the change in character of the New York City population resulting from the trend to the suburbs, the competition from the tabloid morning papers, the keen competition in the news and entertainment area from radio and television, the number of failures and forced mergers of newspapers in other cities in recent years, the strength and aggressiveness of the labor unions in the newspaper field (the *Tribune*'s employees are divided among twelve different unions), the age of much of the *Tribune*'s plant, the great prestige of the *Times* and the momentum it has gained since the War, as well as its alleged willingness to forego large profits in order better to carry out its public service responsibilities, the loss of circulation felt by the *World Telegram* after its increase to 10 cents—all these things would seem to warrant a gloomy appraisal of the odds against the *Tribune*.[23]

Despite these dire warnings Whitney made an initial investment of $1.2 million in the paper and would eventually become its majority owner. To help cover the losses at the *Herald Tribune*, Whitney amassed a collection of other media properties including the New York radio station WINS, as well as a small chain of newspapers and a radio station in Huntington, West Virginia. It would later add the Corinthian Broadcasting Corporation, owner of five television stations and two radio stations scattered around the country, and the VIP Network, which owned four radio stations in the suburbs of New York, and renamed J.H. Whitney & Co. the Whitney Communications Corporation (WCC).[24] In the first year of his ownership, the city's papers closed for the 1958 deliverer's strike, leaving the *Herald Tribune* with a $2 million loss for the year. The strike of 1963 left the paper $4.2 million in the red at the year's end.[25]

One solution under serious consideration was to become an afternoon paper and enter into a joint venture with the *New York Times* by sharing their production facilities. The *Times* would have the morning field to itself and would see its circulation rise dramatically, and the *Tribune* would save considerably in labor costs. However, the proposal did not survive past the death of *Times* publisher Orvil Dryfoos in 1963; when Arthur O. Sulzberger took over the paper he ended negotiations with the *Herald Tribune* altogether. The *Herald Tribune* survived in the short term, and in its few remaining years substantially improved its coverage. The book review section began to challenge the *Times*'s version, and the Sunday magazine, *New York*, initiated a bold new experimental writing style of crafting nonfiction stories using fiction techniques that would come to be known as New Journalism. A new series was undertaken to challenge Mayor Robert F. Wagner Jr.'s leadership in the hope of preventing his fourth term in office. "New York City in Crisis" began in 1965 and provided a platform for John Lindsay to win the election. When the Newspaper Guild struck the *New York Times* for twenty-five days that year, it left the *Herald Tribune* as the only quality morning paper, and circulation rose to almost one million copies a day, the highest it had ever reached.

Once again, however, when the union contracts came up for renewal in 1965, the same issues stymied publishers. If pressrooms were going to automate, union members wanted a share of the profit from the savings. Publishers wanted higher levels of productivity and the right to install technology that required fewer operators, and printers wanted increased hourly wages, a shorter workweek, and more paid vacation. This time, the *New York Times* decided to settle with the unions, perhaps in the hope that the wage increase and the barriers to automation would cause more harm to their competitors than it would to them.

Facing months of lost revenue, the *World-Telegram*, which in 1950 absorbed the *New York Sun* to become the *World Telegram & Sun*, added the *Journal American* and the *Herald Tribune* to become the *World Journal Tribune* in 1966. This was seven papers tracing their history to the nineteenth century now reduced to one. The plan was to publish the *Herald Tribune* as a morning paper, the *World Journal* as an afternoon paper, and the *World Journal Tribune* as a Sunday paper. The new configuration was to be owned equally by the Hearst Corporation, Scripps Howard, and the WCC. In announcing the deal, W. R. Hearst Jr., Jock Whitney, and Jack Howard wrote that "the consolidation into a single company will permit us to achieve substantial cost savings through elimination of duplicating and overlapping functions and by combining production facilities, for the present primarily in one of our three plants and ultimately in one new modern printing facility which we will build."[26] The dream of a new plant would never materialize, however, and the newly merged paper barely got the chance to see if it would succeed because the Newspaper Guild struck before its planned first day on April 24, 1966, arguing that no member had any contract with an entity known as "World Journal Tribune." The other nine unions refused to cross the picket lines at the *World Telegram & Sun* at 125 Barclay, and at the Herald Tribune and Journal American Buildings. Far from functioning as an advertising platform for their businesses, the image of the newspaper building in the late 1960s conjured in the public mind was now simply one of picket lines.

The strike lasted 140 days, the longest in American journalism to that point, but before it could be settled, the *Herald Tribune* closed permanently. The *Washington Post* and the *New York Times*, together with Whitney's WCC, bought the *International Herald Tribune*, and the *New York Post* won the right to bid for the *Herald Tribune*'s syndicated features and columnists. *New York Magazine* was revived as a stand-alone magazine edited by Clay Felker, with writers Gloria Steinem, Tom Wolfe, Pete Hamill, and Jimmy Breslin. Another strike publication, the *New York Review of Books*, that was printed to compensate for the lack of reviews being published during the 1962 strike, continued beyond the strike to become a successful publication.

When the *World Journal Tribune* finally started, it was printed out of 125 Barclay, with the Sunday edition printed out of the former Herald Tribune building on West 40th. The many-headed beast found little favor with readers who had witnessed the evisceration of formerly strong and independent news organizations. It lasted until May 6, 1967, and with its closure eliminated the papers formerly known as the *New York Herald*, the *New-York Tribune*, the *New York World*, the *New York Evening Journal*, the *New York Evening Telegram*, and the *New York Sun*. As the *New York Times* wrote of Barclay Street, "Some 40 men gathered and just stood silently, looking at the 10-story building, as though by scanning its brick exterior they could discern a reason for the paper's demise."[27]

Needless to say, in this period of radical consolidation and labor strife, little was built on the skyline to advertise the news industry. Several new printing facilities were erected in the suburban areas so that papers could be produced closer to their out-of-town-doorstep destinations and amidst union conditions more favorable to newspaper owners. But this postwar suburbanization was also a main factor fueling the industry's disintegration. Papers struggled to stay relevant to the concerns of suburbanites and to expend resources to cover far-strewn localities. New papers like *Newsday* on Long Island had emerged to cater to the growing population in Suffolk and Nassau Counties, and department stores and their advertising went with them.

## New York Post

Dorothy Schiff had taken possession of the *New York Post* from J. David Stern, who acquired it after Cyrus Curtis's death in 1933. Stern had succeeded in shifting the paper back to its former Democratic orientation, and thought it could be a useful tool for supporting the New Deal along with his other holdings, the *Philadelphia Record* and Camden (New Jersey) *Courier-Post*. Unable to keep all three going at one time, in 1939 he sold the *New York Post* to George Backer and Dorothy Schiff, who was married to Backer. Although the marriage did not last, Schiff would take over as the *Post*'s president and publisher and would run the paper for thirty-seven years before selling it to Rupert Murdoch in 1976. Metropolitan Life owned the building at 75 West Street that Curtis had built and where the *Post* remained for forty-five years, with Schiff occupying the elegantly appointed seventeenth-floor penthouse office, earning her the title, "The Lady Upstairs."

Schiff thought that her liberal paper, paradoxically, made it a more glaring target for strikers because liberal papers were more likely to be struggling financially and more vulnerable. During the 114-day newspaper strike of 1962–63 that closed the *Daily Mirror* permanently, Schiff renounced her membership in the New York Publishers Association on the eighty-third day so that she was not held to their collective bargaining rules. She restarted the presses four days later. As she wrote in an editorial, "It has been their strategy to pick the newspaper most sympathetic to labor to use as an instrument to set the scale for the entire industry. They do this because usually these are the weakest papers financially, therefore least able to stand a strike. Why are the liberal newspapers apt to be poor? Because many big advertisers are reluctant to help build a medium which they believe has an editorial policy adversely affecting their special interests."[28]

But for the weeks that the *Post* was publishing while the others were not, the paper made significant gains in circulation that gave it hope. It was printing 600,000 copies a day and advertisers needed it to keep in touch with readers. By the time of the 1962–63 strike, however, radio and television were far more developed than they had been during earlier strikes, and the habit developed of receiving broadcast news during the prolonged strike was not easily broken when the papers returned. Facing these new challenges, papers had to work to woo back their readers. Among the strategies employed by the *New York Post* was to work with, rather than against, television by devoting more attention to it in the form of listings and articles in a new eight-page section.

The paper was said to be oriented toward urban, largely Jewish, liberals. When in 1959 the subject of printing stock tables in the paper came up, editor James Wechsler replied, "I have no principled objection to stock tables, but I fear that the issue lies between those of us here (mostly myself) who regard the *Post's* liberal identification as its reason for existence and those who would like to make it more congenial to the increasingly conservative . . . middle class of suburbia."[29] That the *Post* was committed to the liberal metropolitan reader was reflected in the crusading urbanity of its coverage. It maintained a close eye on local sports, schools, and politics, ran in-depth investigative journalism, and had a strong and singular editorial voice—which could not be said of the conglomerate *World Journal Tribune* where too many editorial traditions were attempting to fuse as one.

Journal American Building, then Post Building, at 220 South Street. The New York Public Library, Astor, Lenox and Tilden Foundations)

When that paper closed, and with no competition in the afternoon field left, the *Post* was able to expand its circulation from 345,000 in 1965 to 700,000 in 1967. Its presses at 75 West Street were operating at maximum capacity, so the decision was made to buy the block-long building on South Street left empty after the demise of Hearst's *Journal American*.[30] Although the climate of newspaper consolidation in the 1960s did little to augment the architecture of the industry, the closing of the *World Journal Tribune* did provide Dorothy Schiff with the necessary confidence in the *Post* to invest in its future.

In preparation for the move to the former Hearst building in 1967, Schiff paid $1.5 million for the land and the six-story building that occupied the entire block bordered by South Street, Water Street, Catherine Slip, and Market Slip. The move in 1970 took place amidst the recession hitting New York, and the price for the property appeared to be a great bargain. On closer inspection, however, it became clear that its isolated location and the necessary renovations required to fortify the building for new presses and other equipment justified the low price. By the end of the relocation, over $10 million had been spent. But with new presses (including four four-color Goss presses, able to print 70,000 copies an hour), the paper could expand to 120 pages with pages two inches wider to accommodate six rather than five columns per page.[31]

Schiff's approach to the new structure illustrated a radical change in the governing logic of news buildings. Against the prevailing notion that architecture could be used as a permanent billboard for the paper it housed, Schiff chose a location that had already shown itself to be inconveniently located to pedestrian traffic, and made all the more so by the construction of the elevated lanes of the East River Drive (now FDR Drive) that opened to traffic directly in front of the building in 1954. When the subject of signage on the building's front was raised, Schiff was unequivocal. Her executive editor Paul Sann suggested that "we need something on the roof, but in big type, that says it's the New York Post. It shouldn't cost an awful lot." Schiff replied, "You know that we have no sign on the façade of the building indicating that it's the New York Post. This is because of the danger of vandalism. There would be some danger these days in having our name on the roof of the building. Some unfriendly person might be tempted to drop a bomb."[32] Where other buildings in the field announced their presence boldly with signature architecture, outsized lettering, and other design features that matched the internal operations to the building's façade, Schiff worried about being a target for destructive action by opponents. Having endured numerous grievances by workers and several fires in the pressrooms at 75 West Street, her ambivalence toward corporate visibility seemed sound.

Although the South Street New York Post building was not a new building, or even a new news building, it was to be the last meaningful architectural event in the industry for some time. A mass movement of corporate headquarters out of Manhattan followed the simultaneous recession and inflation of the 1970s, making the idea of new architectural showpieces somewhat counterintuitive. As Miriam Greenberg has written, "When combined with the increasing rate of corporate mergers in the period of restructuring, by 1974 New York City had a net loss of between seventy-six and eighty-eight of the nation's most important headquarters, as well as tens of smaller firms and with them thousands of high-end service jobs. The gain to New York's local suburbs was massive—between 1968 and 1974, they tripled their share of Fortune 500 companies while New York lost 30 percent of its share."[33]

Increased crime and taxes left only 94 of the Fortune 500 headquarters in the city in 1975, down from 125 in 1970.[34] A deteriorating school system impacted the quality of the workforce, while executives preferred to work out of new offices in New Jersey and Connecticut, closer to where they lived and where the transportation infrastructure and local crime posed fewer challenges. New York's own fiscal crisis, a result of mounting debt and expenditures that outstripped tax income, nearly bankrupted the city more than once. Mayor Abe Beame blamed the city's newspapers for "creating an atmosphere of doubt and uncertainty" whenever they reported on the fiscal situation; and when President Gerald Ford announced that no federal help would be forthcoming, the *Daily News* famously issued its full front page headline: "Ford to City: Drop Dead."[35]

As in the nineteenth century, it would be a bank that would resume the height competition in corporate architecture. After several fallow years, the Citicorp Building on Lexington at 53rd Street topped out in October 1976 at 914 feet. Still slightly shy of the very tips of the Chrysler and Empire State Buildings, and with fewer floors than the twin towers of the World Trade Center, it would nevertheless claim the title as the city's third, and the world's seventh, tallest building—a remarkable feat in an era when so many companies were fleeing rather than breaking ground in Manhattan. That this new structure would usher in a new era of corporate building in the city presaged the increasing interpenetration of the media and banking industries, as Greenberg notes:

Business services took advantage of media's growth, becoming deeply involved in film, TV and new media activities at many levels. Banks began taking equity positions in media and entertainment ventures, accounting firms began creating entertainment or media divisions, and investment houses began handling media- and entertainment-related stocks and bond offerings on a far larger scale. By the late 1980s, with the stock market crash and the onset of recession, media and entertainment caught up with business services to become New York's fastest growing sector, and its firms some of the biggest political and economic actors in the city.[36]

The city that had seen the consolidation of twenty-five newspapers in 1900 into six by 1965, none of which were operating on Park Row,[37] would re-emerge in the twenty-first century as the headquarters of a global media industry, bringing with it a new architecture of media conglomeration.

# Epilogue

On the eve of the inauguration of President Barack Obama in 2008, one of the largest parties was hosted by the *Huffington Post* at the Newseum in Washington, D.C. That a website, and not a legacy media company like the *Washington Post*, held the night's most high-profile gala struck many in the crowd as a sign of the potency of the social media that had helped propel the new president into the White House. Three years later, the *Huffington Post* made headlines again with the announcement that it was being sold to America Online (AOL). A generation earlier, it would have seemed inconceivable that AOL, known primarily as an Internet service provider, would be considered *media*.

In January 2000, when AOL and Time Warner announced their intention to merge, the most troubling aspect of the deal was not that old media was pairing up with new media, but that it was the upstart AOL that was purchasing the stalwart Time Warner, a company five times its size. The agreement made a great deal of sense "on paper," which was to say that although AOL did not have nearly the tangible assets of Time Warner, if valued correctly its stock price could make it appear to be worth more. The investment bank leading the deal successfully convinced both companies that with AOL's pipeline into American homes, and Time Warner's sizeable content catalog, myriad unrealized economies of scale and synergies could be achieved. In practice, however, the new company was not able to merge quite so seamlessly.

The merger announcement was accompanied by news of a new corporate headquarters in Midtown Manhattan. Construction began a month later and the building was completed in 2003. The new project, to be named One Columbus Circle, had as its defining feature two "twin" 750-foot towers. The symbolism was both rich and unsettling. Said to echo the twin-towered luxury apartment buildings lining Central Park West like the San Remo, the Eldorado, and the Century Apartments, by the time these towers went up they more stirringly evoked the phantom presence of the twin towers at the World Trade Center destroyed in the terrorist attacks of September 11, 2001. Much speculation surrounded the fitness of the tall-tower model in

New York: the fear of creating another target competed with an exuberant defiance of terrorism. Understanding how these two sentiments would be reconciled was essential to those attempting to secure tenants for the towers.

The developer need not have worried. Before long the condominiums in the tower were commanding the highest prices per square foot anywhere in Manhattan. Despite housing condominiums and hotel rooms, not corporate offices, the towers nevertheless were seen as evidence of two moguls of media strength standing side by side. The public perception of the towers was that these two soaring spires were the physical embodiment of old and new media coming together on equal footing; one tower for Time Warner and the other for AOL. But even in jest the design of this building had little to do with a strategy to communicate a smooth merger to the public. The developer, Related Companies, had been negotiating with Time Warner as early as 1998, well in advance of the merger with AOL. But as Steve Ross of Related Companies recalled telling Time Warner's Richard Parsons, "This is a great way to present yourself to the world. . . . This is branding, which is what the 21st century is all about."[1] When Parsons replied that the company already had enough space at Rockefeller Center, Ross rehearsed the lesson of the last two centuries of media architecture: "It's not about space, it's about showcasing your company!"[2] While the structure worked to convey the idea of the merged entity to the public, as a showcase it carried all of the attendant risks and consequences of corporate visibility.

For many people, including AOL Time Warner stockholders, journalists, and members of the general public, the grand twin-towered skyscraper at Columbus Circle would stand as a testament to a failed attempt to merge old media with new; a gleaming new set of towers on a prestige site that, in light of the plummeting stock price of the new company, mocked the hubris that led to one of the least successful mergers in recent memory. One stockholder was widely reported to exclaim at the company's general meeting his dismay that the "Taj Mahal at Columbus Circle" was being financed on the backs of stockholders like himself.[3] With land purchased from the Metropolitan Transit Authority for $357 million and a building cost of an estimated $1.6 billion, the structure was a painful reminder of how much value both AOL and Time Warner had lost.

The enormous growth of the stock market that occurred in the 1990s meant that far more people than at any time in American history considered themselves "investors," and as a consequence these prominent corporate symbols in architecture resonated well beyond the insular world of investment bankers and board members. The financial euphoria of the late '90s that encouraged expanded participation through mutual funds, discount brokerages, and online trading brought many new sources of revenue into play, especially for technology companies. It was in this context that AOL and Time Warner saw fit to merge, and against the backdrop of the burst bubble that their new headquarters was viewed. It was such accusations of profligacy that earlier media entities worked to forestall. Their tall towers did not read to the public as wasteful because so few members of the public had money at stake. Shareholders could grumble at the folly of raising capital to build a monument in the sky, but the risk was confined to a handful of relatively financially secure men. By comparison, the Time Warner building was a complex financial instrument with numerous stakeholders. Early in 2003, the California Public Employees' Retirement System (CALPERS), the largest pension fund in the country, made an investment that gave it 49.5 percent of the building.[4]

While most of the attention was focused on the towers—their parallelo-gram shape cutting at an angle to make them align with Manhattan's grid without blocking light or creating unnecessary shadow—it was the forms below the towers that were of most interest to the Time Warner Company. Between the retail area and the two towers are two midrise buildings for live studio and office spaces, including live broadcast production studios for CNN. This was the portion of the building that was to integrate the vastly different corporate cultures of AOL and Time Warner. But despite all of the publicity generated to promote the building-as-merger symbolism, the new corporate headquarters was never home to AOL. Even before the building was fully occupied, the company spent $500,000 removing the AOL name from its logo on all corporate material, including the front of the building.[5] Plans for a three-level, 43,000-square-foot, AOL-branded interactive space were eliminated from the original sketches in the shopping area known as the Palladium,[6] and before the decade was out the company would split up entirely.

The building's design nevertheless evokes more than a century of me-dia architecture in New York. Constructed as a space for public gathering on a prominent square, it can easily be viewed as the continuation of the northward expansion of the media industry beginning with William Ran-dolph Hearst's plans to make Columbus Circle the next media landmark after Herald Square and Times Square. David Childs, the architect from Skidmore Owings & Merrill in charge of the design, conceived the structure

Time Warner Center
at Columbus Circle.
(Time Warner)

as a complex multifunction center for living, shopping, entertainment, and corporate use. This orientation reflects not only a contemporary approach to land development that seeks to maximize traffic by incorporating different populations using the space at different times of day, but also signals the reemergence of media headquarters as destinations. That such media spaces are now largely imagined as spaces of consumption rather than information gathering is a legacy of the development of Times Square, where media-sponsored entertainment and spectacle reach their apotheosis.

At the Time Warner Center, studios for CNN broadcast live and the location on Central Park establishes the corporate claim to the centrality of media production in contrast to its more peripheral Atlanta studios. But like the Time Warner Center in Atlanta, the overriding design logic of the structure is that of a mall, a space for branding the network alongside many other competing brands. The public does not gather at the building to participate in news. The skyscraper mall is a total, interiorized environment that mirrors the virtual world of online commerce. There is no retail outlet that does not also have an online presence, and there is no built destination that cannot also be accessed via a website. As *Wired* magazine wrote, invoking the conflation, "To sign on to AOL is to enter the cyber version of a suburban mall—a carefully modulated, vaguely cutesy-poo environment where the ambience is serenely antiseptic (as long as you don't venture into the wrong chat room late at night) and the impulse to consume is stimulated at every stop. For a lot of people that's great, at least when the system isn't jammed with too many users fighting over too little infrastructure. But the Web, with its wide-open electronic boulevards and anything-goes mystique, lies just a click away."[7]

## The Hearst Building, Continued

Although Hearst did not live to see his eponymous tower built in Manhattan, and was not able to secure a site at Columbus Circle, in 2006 a Hearst Tower was finally erected on a foundation built in 1928. During the 1920s Hearst purchased so many plots of land in Midtown for possible use as headquarters that contemporaries and business associates could be forgiven for not knowing exactly what he had in mind. Among the ideas was a 57th Street corridor, owned by Hearst, that would be the central passageway across Manhattan should a bridge over the Hudson ever be built at that location. Another was the establishment of a "Hearst Plaza" overtaking all of Columbus Circle, although he also purchased the Essex Hotel on the East Side as a potential site for his enterprises.

The only plan ever realized, however, was the one Hearst commissioned from Joseph Urban to house his magazine interests. Urban was a leading theater designer, and notably the set designer for Florenz Ziegfeld, whose "Follies" occasioned the appearance of Hearst's longtime mistress, Marion Davies. Continuing his collaboration with Hearst, Urban remodeled the Criterion and Cosmopolitan Theaters to improve Davies's backdrop. The six-story Hearst structure was but a base of a building, anticipating a larger tower above; a stage, designed by a stage crafter. Given Hearst's professional and personal interest in the theater, his choice of location is not surprising. Plans for the Metropolitan Opera had been announced on a site next to the Magazine Building on 57th, and Urban had been commissioned as its architect as well. It was this orientation that led Hearst to seek not general moral uplift from his building, but rather something more specifically cultural: "It was designed with an auditorium for concerts, lectures and similar educational activities," its elaborate building program was "a stylistic synthesis of Art Deco ornament, Secessionist influence and Baroque theatricality."[8] Echoing Pulitzer's World Building, with its Truth, Justice, Art, Literature, Science, and Invention torchbearers, the Viennese modernism of Robert Kohn's 1906 Evening Post Building, with its allegorical statues depicting the Four Periods of Publicity, and the frieze on the façade of the Daily News Building with its working men and women of New York, the limestone base of Urban's building portrays "a bare-torsoed athlete holding a discus and a hard-hatted workman resting on his sledgehammer represent[ing] Sport and Industry; a jester in a fool's cap and a gloom-ridden tragedian depict[ing] Comedy and Tragedy; a musician with a lyre and a statue in classical armor stand[ing] for Music and Art; and a bearded man with an iron press and a cowled woman with two owls stand[ing] for Printing and Sciences."[9]

The base, according to Eric Nash, was "a charmingly literal interpretation of the aspirations of the Hearst empire in theater and communications."[10] In the tradition of publishers who saw fit to editorialize on the merits of superior architecture just as their own buildings were in planning stages, Hearst primed the pump with this paean:

> New York is developing the most magnificent architecture in the world— an architecture that is not an imitation of some other period, a modification of some other type, but that is new and distinctly American in character. This architecture represents the energy, the imagination and the aspiration of the American spirit. It embodies the ambition of a great race to erect fitting monuments to its period and purposes. . . . Those who are truly artistic, truly progressive and indeed truly patriotic, welcome this new and inspiring development. . . . The old fogies, the back numbers, the "has-beens," the live-in-the-past-dead-in-the-present contingent of obstructionists must not be allowed to control, or rather to prevent, the natural and national development of American architecture.[11]

All of which was to say that if the public did not favor his new Magazine Building when it was finished, it would be because they were backward, unpatriotic louts. Before his death Hearst ended up selling a great many of the pieces of land he acquired in his more flush days, and it did not escape the notice of a profile writer in the *New Yorker* that "in the chief cities of the country there are no great 'Hearst Squares'—huge buildings from which his publications were to be issued and go on forever, veritable mausoleums of steel and stone."[12]

The International Magazine Building, at 57th Street and Eighth Avenue was landmarked in 1987, long before any realistic plan for expansion was afoot, and so any attempt to build on the site had to incorporate at least the façade of the structure. Lord Norman Foster's forty-six-story glass-and-steel skyscraper therefore nests inside the shell of Urban's walls, creating an open ground-level lobby that maintains its connection with the company's storied past. In emptying out the original building, the architect was said to evoke both a traditional town square and a civic building in the mode of the Italian Renaissance, well-established templates for media buildings since the nineteenth century. "Traditionally, as you approach a classical building, you ascend the steps and go up to the principal level," what he calls the *piano nobile* or noble floor.[13]

Foster had established a reputation as an architect able to take historic structures and amend them with modern design, as he did at the Reichstag

International Magazine Building, Joseph Urban, 1928. (Columbia University)

in Berlin and the British Museum court in London. The interplay of old and new in the Hearst Building recalls Pulitzer's use of the terms "Old World" and "New World" on Park Row (see chapter 3). Joseph Urban's original pedestal for the new building allowed the Hearst Corporation, one of the few remaining media companies with a solid claim to its continuity over the previous century, to convey both tradition and future growth potential at the same time.

The $500 million project did not, as was the case at Time Warner, raise the ire of the public because the Hearst Corporation is a privately held company. As an entirely owner-occupied structure, the mandate to maximize the rentable square footage was less strict. Here, diagonal cutouts at the corners provide light and angled views and the lost portions of the floor plate are not a concern. Although many efficiencies are realized in a building that brings together all of the company's operations under one roof instead of renting office space in far-flung locations, the gain is also found in branding symbolism. Because many of the company's magazines—including *Esquire, Cosmopolitan, Good Housekeeping, House Beautiful, Country Living, Harper's Bazaar,* and *Marie Claire*—cohere around fashion, beauty, and lifestyle, having them housed in a structure that is photogenic and visually unique is a sound strategy. As with all media architecture, the intended interpretation is given best through the company's own products. In the case of the Hearst Building, the narrative is anchored to the ominous timing of Foster's meeting to present his plans for the new tower: September 12, 2001. Thus "courage" and "resilience" figure in an editorial in *Harper's Bazaar,* but the refrain that would become inseparable from the building was that provided by one of the other Hearst magazines, *Popular Mechanics*: "Rising among the staid rectangular buildings of midtown Manhattan is an anomaly in the urban landscape: a sleek, faceted skyscraper glittering above a squat, ornate plinth. Architecture critic Paul Goldberger calls the new Hearst Tower the most beautiful addition to the city skyline in 40 years. But accolades extend beyond the curtain wall: Cutting-edge engineering makes it a model of sustainable design."[14]

Here "green" or "sustainable" design has usurped height as the index of achievement for media buildings in the twenty-first century. After its main competitor in the magazine field, Condé Nast, established sustainability as the preferred measure of its building at 4 Times Square,[15] Hearst had little choice but to follow suit. Appeals to environmentalism help compensate for an industry still largely delivered on paper in addition to fitting well with the contemporary ethos, providing both energy and excellent public relations value. The structure's four-story triangular frames "eliminated the need for approximately 2,000 tons of steel" and the building publicity emphasizes that "foreign-sourced materials account for less than 10% of the total cost of construction."[16]

In the post-9/11 atmosphere, decreased reliance on foreign goods and reduced energy consumption stand in stark contrast to the celebrations of the surplus economy lauded by earlier generations. The Hearst Tower boasts that it is the first "green" office building in New York City, a claim supported by the fact that "90% of the Tower's structural steel contains recycled materials," and that its "roof collects rainwater, reducing the amount of water dumped into the city's sewer system during rainfall by 25%."[17] Using the recycled water for its lobby waterfall helps to cool the temperature and provide moisture in dry months.[18] Where the tall building was once lauded

Hearst Building, Norman Foster, 2007. (Hearst Corporation)

for its civic virtue by providing an aspirational model and symbol of success for city residents, the appeal to environmentalism conveys ecological stewardship and corporate social responsibility. Working to allay charges of arrogance and excess in an age of corporate malfeasance, the green building has become one of the few acceptable means of corporate self-presentation in architecture, while providing further marketing support for the brand.

## The New *New York Times*

Echoing the side-by-side comparisons of competitors in the previous century, the building process of the Hearst Building was taking place against the also-rising New York Times Building sixteen blocks south on 8th Avenue. Several commentators noted at the time that they would be watching each other closely to see which design would gain the public's favor, and whether the Times Building would meet the new standard of environmentalism set by Hearst.[19] Indeed, its exterior walls are constructed of horizontal ceramic rods that reduce energy use inside by responding to external weather and light conditions that automatically adjust the interior settings. Besting the Hearst Tower, more than 95 percent of the structural steel is made from recycled material. Yet height remains as important to the design as it has for all previous Times towers—at 1,064 feet, the building is much taller than it needs to be to house the paper's operations. Since printing is no longer done on the premises of most newspaper buildings, the heavy floor plates at ground level that previously held presses and allowed for delivery bays are not part of the design plan. What replaces these spaces are open areas for meeting, collaboration, atria, and cafeterias; design elements borrowed from the new corporate culture found in suburban work compounds like those at Google, Nike, Amazon, and AOL, all of which occupy out-of-the-way sprawling complexes. The Times Building's interior attempts to level hierarchy with open plan designs, and where there are office walls they are made of glass.

Adding interest was the fact that two of the world's most celebrated architects were competing: Lord Norman Foster was up against Renzo Piano. Foster, Piano, David Childs, Frank Gehry, and Cesar Pelli were all sent invitations to apply for the Times Building commission. The prospectus informed applicants of Herbert Muschamp's view that "*Architecture*, like journalism, is a daring form of knowing. It depends on a willingness to risk the unknown."[20] Italian architect Renzo Piano, the coarchitect of the Pompidou Center in Paris, was selected, and the *Times* enthusiastically extolled the decision on its front page. In Piano's words, architecture is "about making buildings, but it is also about telling stories, and the story I hope this building tells is not about arrogance and power. I hope this building will tell a story about transparency and lightness."[21] Working with the firm Fox and Fowle, who had previously built the new media skyscrapers at Times Square housing Condé Nast and Reuters, the building was destined to be more digital than analog in orientation.

Where all previous Times towers emphasized stability, strength, fortitude, and permanence, Piano's tower stresses transparency, reflection, and adaptability. But the new building responds to current mandates as much as the newspaper buildings of one hundred years ago did to theirs: the new glass-walled New York Times Building is an architectural rejoinder to the scandals that had befallen the paper. Where the former homes of the *Times* were stone monuments to power and permanence—reminders that serious, important work was going on inside—these walls invite the public's scrutiny of the paper, a scrutiny grown more intense in no small part by the

New York Times Building, Renzo Piano, 2008. (© Peter Mauss/Esto)

electronic mode of communication that has posed such a challenge to the business. In spring 2003, reporter Jayson Blair was accused of plagiarism and having reported stories he did not investigate. After his resignation an internal investigation by *Times* reporters was published, and among the recommendations were strategies to deflect concern that the paper could no longer be held up as the standard bearer of trustworthy news. As a result of this inquiry, the paper instituted Daniel Okrent as public editor and to be an internal ombudsperson, and Allan Siegal as standards editor, charged with the task of training reporters in fact-checking, accuracy, and ethics. The internal investigation also led to a corporate reshuffling, a public acknowledgment of wrongdoing, and an apology. At a paper whose own legacy opened it up to criticism that it could not be relevant to a new generation of readers—that its history and its size prevented it from being nimble enough to be on top of truly breaking cultural stories and phenomena—this series of changes signaled something significant indeed.

Part of the building's design philosophy was to break down the barrier between the paper and the city, both materially and symbolically. The operations of the *Times* are on view from the outside, and the city is made more immediate from the inside. As Piano claimed, "We looked at the organization of the *New York Times*. The paper takes from the city to feed its editorial machine, and then gives something back to the city. As its motto says, 'All the News that's Fit to Print.' We wanted to create a building that made New York and the *Times* somehow one and the same thing."[22] The building is the company's attempt to make its continued relevance in the digital media environment legible on the skyline, and Piano references this paradox of dematerialization: "As newspapers become less tangible creations, I think they need special buildings of their own to root them in the world of the everyday, to connect them physically with their readers, and to give journalists themselves a place to roost."[23]

Employing its own paper to provide the preferred interpretation of the structure, the *New York Times* used its significant voice on matters of design, taste, and agenda-setting to explain its new home. The rhetoric attached to the new Times Building by both Piano and by the paper's architecture critics imbued the new building with self-satisfied hope. As Herbert Muschamp, then architecture critic at the paper and a member of the selection committee, wrote in the *Times*, "What Piano brings to the job, apart from his talent, is a deeply ingrained sense of civic responsibility, a conviction that the *Times* must give back, through *architecture*, the good fortune it has enjoyed."[24] Finding Piano "a great poet of circulation," words like "vibration," "breathing," and "magic" are used to describe the building. These are, according to Piano, "the immaterials of architecture." For the Times Tower, he described a "triple skin wall that lifts the material city's grid into a metaphysical realm." In the architectural realm, as Muschamp put it, "The newsroom reaches daily toward the Enlightenment ideals of free speech and independent inquiry, however imperfectly. The newsroom itself, as well as its coverage of news, has been powerfully affected by debates over authority that have unfolded in *architecture* and throughout the culture. The paper has the responsibility to challenge and correct, not blindly affirm, the corporate world's view of itself."[25]

And yet time and again the role of the paper as a news agenda setter and the role of corporate developer have been at odds. In 1985 the *Times* fought an attempt by the Landmarks Preservation Commission to designate its 43rd Street building a city landmark. As a cultural institution it should have wanted the status, but as real estate investors it did not want anything that might make the sale of the property more difficult. The Landmark Commission did not pursue a lengthy battle, fearing that they would be on the losing end of a publicity fight. In assembling the land for its new building, eminent domain was invoked to get the existing buildings taken down—a student dorm, many shops, and some restaurants, none of which were "blighted." Editorially the *Times* is routinely against the use of eminent domain—they did not disclose in their pages that they used it themselves to get the land for their new building.

The lease for the new building also included clauses that ran counter to the good stewardship promoted by the *Times*. It was forbidden to rent the space not being used by the *Times* to a school, day care, or drop-in center, welfare or social services office, homeless shelter or homeless assistance center, a court or court-related facilities. It also forbade doctors' and dentists' offices, government offices, or any operation that might be considered controversial or that had the potential to be the focus of demonstrations. It banned any employment agency (except for executive search firms), job-training centers, and auction houses, except for those specializing in art and/or historical artifacts. While these conditions are typical in much corporate real estate, not allowing the public into the building is especially problematic given that to invoke eminent domain "public purpose" must be demonstrated. The *Times* also got tens of millions of dollars in city subsidies based on what it said were the high costs of keeping 750 workers based in New York City instead of New Jersey.

Following the redevelopment of Times Square, where building façades themselves are tourist attractions, new media architecture has sought ways of incorporating media audiences into their plans. At Times Square, the major networks, along with Nasdaq and Thomson Reuters, have all turned their headquarters into street-level studios where news is disseminated by way of scrolling marquees, giant plasma television screens, and live studio audience participation. The *Times* began using the "Motograph News Bulletin" on its fourth-story exterior during the November 1928 elections, allowing a continuous moving text to scroll around the building.[26] Up to that point, bulletin board stereopticons were still used to announce the news during major events, and for elections, a complicated series of lighted semaphores told those without radios who was winning via different colored lightbulbs lit in ascending or descending order. The Motograph remained as a feature of the building following its success during the election, with the paper reporting the next day that it would light up from twilight to midnight each night: "News of local, national and international interest will be flashed direct from the editorial rooms of THE TIMES to the bulletin board when it begins nightly operation, so that all in the neighborhood may read. The bulletins will be news of the world, as fast as telegraph, radio and cable bring the stories to the editorial rooms." Noting that a second level would soon be added, to "double the story-telling capacity of the sign,"[27] this became the *New York Times* not in stone, but in lights. Along with its roof-top beacon, the building was a signpost on the Great White Way, where people gathered to be together to receive important news. The "zipper," as it came to be called, gave form to the new town square. The slim proportions of the 1904 building could not contain the growing news organization, so while the journalists churned out their copy from the Annex on West 43rd Street, the Times Square building performed an entirely promotional role for the paper. It became a pure billboard. As Marshall Berman wrote nostalgically of the scrolling news sign, "It was a terrific ad for the *Times*, telling us that even in the midst of the Square's carnival phantasmagoria, we could trust the paper to keep us in touch with what was going on in the real world. Its electronic power suggested not that newspapers were being superseded by 'new media,' but that this paper was resourceful enough to do whatever it would take to keep the public in touch."[28]

Now, as digitization makes media less and less visible, media companies continue to seek embodiment in the form of showpiece architecture. As content shifts from printed pages, television broadcasts, and radio announcements to the paradoxically intangible yet ubiquitous Internet, architecture has returned to give form to the basic premise that content has a location. Though electronic communication obviates the need for centralized media production and dissemination, built media spaces again dominate the downtowns of the world's largest cities, and New York's skyline remains one of the most important concentrations of signature buildings designed to differentiate industry leaders from their competition. We may be tempted to conclude that such facile attempts at public persuasion through corporate architecture have no place in the twenty-first century era of instantaneous communication and image management. But the building programs of these newest media structures show remarkable continuity with surrounding media structures and with the history of such structures in New York. While other industries have opted for less expensive land and commuter access to highways available in suburban and exurban development zones, legacy media companies are still found in the center of the city. Saskia Sassen demonstrates that the global media industry continues to cluster because "economies occur in such specialized firms when they locate close to others that produce key inputs or whose proximity makes possible joint production of certain service offerings."[29] It is not only the availability of talented workers that makes geographic concentration an economic imperative, but also access to content and finance capital. Midtown locations are just as important for access to the headquarters of Morgan Stanley as they are for proximity to Condé Nast, Viacom, and Bertlesmann. As William Taylor has written, the area around Times Square became a "beacon of journalistic metropolitanism" as early as the 1930s, with the concentration of the *Times*, the *Herald Tribune*, magazine offices, and the bars at the Algonquin and the Royalton Hotels that their employees frequented.[30]

The news of building in the pre-television and pre-Internet era was especially important for determining how people would come to view a company. Newspaper owners knew that their corporate identity was largely formed through the public's experience with the architecture of their company's headquarters, and in the news business they could all but control their own press by setting the terms of debate on any new construction in their own pages. What is striking about the history of older media buildings like the Times Building at Times Square is the value given to the design, intention, and symbolic interpretation of the structure. A singular vision emerges out of the publisher's desire to announce the identity of the business to his public. As was frequently noted at the time, "the Times building is the *New York Times* in stone." Working with an architect and few others, this vision was easily articulated using the newspaper to communicate the preferred interpretation to readers. Once completed, we may presume a certain fixity to both the structure and its meaning for passersby, at least until such time as a new building was deemed necessary. Indeed the justification for the construction of a new headquarters was often as full of self-aggrandizing rhetoric as were the glowing appreciations of the finished product. If media buildings are any indication, the move to a larger structure was presented to the public as an outward sign of the company's stability and healthy growth, even if the company occupied no more space in the new building than they did in the old. The value of the new building was not to be found in the larger interior space, but rather in the currency that the new exterior had for public relations.

While these new media buildings embody many of the characteristics of traditional media architecture—a tall imposing structure on a prestige centralized site, a celebrity architect, and an attempt to convey a coherent symbolic interpretation to the public—they also represent a shift toward something we might call an architecture of conglomeration. The focus of symbolic interpretation has shifted from intention to inhabitation. The emphasis has moved away from the vision of a single media mogul toward a design determined by developers and a large corporate entity with multifaceted product lines and services and an ever-changing management structure. The architecture of conglomeration is the expression of synergy in the built environment, an attempt to integrate a wide array of commercial entities in such a way that they support each other. In attempting to serve both media past and media future, it must balance a new set of conditions in urban and virtual space—occupation by diverse and highly developed work cultures—and the competing interests of new media ventures in old media space.

## New Media in Old Media Space

In a remarkable reversal that could not have been predicted by the media industry leaders who sought to concentrate their operations in Midtown Manhattan over the course of the twentieth century, the area surrounding Park Row is now reemerging as a site for media production. Where once news buildings and bank buildings vied for height supremacy, and then for proximity to each other, the latest building plans in Manhattan place the *Daily News* and American Media, publisher of the *National Enquirer* and health and fitness magazines, inside the former JP Morgan Chase building at 4 New York Plaza in lower Manhattan. In the nineteenth century banks and newspapers occupied strikingly similar forms but advertised to much different ends. Both built tall but their appeals to civic life and corporate prowess distinguished their interpretations. Now, automated web-based labor makes it possible for these industries to occupy each other's spaces. The *Daily News* will be joined by the magazine conglomerate Condé Nast, which will occupy space as an anchor tenant at 1 World Trade Center, the 1,776-foot building replacing the former World Trade Center. Mansueto Ventures, which publishes *Inc.* and *Fast Company*, are located at 7 World Trade Center. *U.S. News and World Report*, *The Daily Beast*, and *Newsweek* will also locate nearby. There will be no printing presses in the basement and no typewriters on the desks, but Wall Street and City Hall will be close at hand just as they were in the nineteenth century.[31]

# Notes

INTRODUCTION

1. *New York Times*, "Towers of Babel," March 7, 1920, E2.
2. Lippman, *Public Opinion*, 162.
3. Ibid., 340.
4. Hobsbawm, *The Invention of Tradition.*
5. Ibid., 2.
6. Marchand, *Advertising the American Dream*, xx.
7. Taylor, "The Evolution of Public Space in New York City," 291.
8. Marchand, *Creating the Corporate Soul.*
9. Marquis, *The Metropolitan Life*, 15.
10. Shachtman, *Skyscraper Dreams*, 50.
11. McGurl, "Making it Big," 417.
12. In print advertising, the long thin ads that ran down the side of pages came to be known as "skyscrapers," a language still used to describe vertical ads that run down the length of newspaper websites.
13. Bessie, *Jazz Journalism.*
14. Eco, "Function and Sign."

CHAPTER I. NEWS CAPITAL

1. O'Brien, *The Story of the Sun*, 30.
2. Jackson, *The Great Metropolis*, 1.
3. Warner, *The Letters of the Republic*, 18.
4. Lindner, *The Reportage of Urban Culture*, 70.
5. Glaab and Brown, *The History of Urban America*, 139–40.
6. Carey, "Technology and Ideology," 305.
7. Ibid., 315.
8. See Schudson, *Discovering the News.*
9. Barth, *City People*, 59.
10. O'Brien, *The Story of the Sun*, 24.
11. Quoted in ibid., 39.
12. Published in the *New York Sun*, August and September 1835.
13. *New York Sun*, January 27, 1868. Dana also kept the two-cent price, the original format of four pages, and the slogan, "It Shines for All." For editorial and news quality, the *Sun* was widely understood throughout to be the leader among the plethora of news organs in New York. Under Dana, it was also the best-written newspaper in the city, with reporters working under threat of termination for the slightest grammatical error.

14. Janet Steele has noted that the takeover of the Tammany Hall building had the unfortunate consequence of equating the *Sun* with Tammany in the public mind, adding that "the Republican press charged that the so-called Tweed ring purchased newspaper support with payoffs to reporters in return for favorable blurbs." Steele, *The Sun Shines for All*, 153.

15. Lancaster, *Gentleman of the Press*, 69.

16. Quoted in Stone, *Dana and "The Sun*," 53. Pulitzer was the *Sun's* Washington correspondent in 1867.

17. Kennion, *The Architects' and Builders' Guide*, 60.

18. Steele, *The Sun Shines for All*, 119.

19. *New York Sun*, February 8, 1891, 16.

20. Van Leeuwen, *Skyward Trend of Thought*, 109.

21. Quoted in Seitz, *The James Gordon Bennetts*, 39.

22. Ibid., 75.

23. Browne, *The Great Metropolis*, 5.

24. Pray, *Memoirs of James Gordon Bennett*, 194.

25. Crouthamel, *Bennett's New York Herald*, 20.

26. Seitz, *The James Gordon Bennetts*, 119.

27. *New York Herald*, August 27, 1845, 1.

28. Ibid.

29. Bennett, *New York Herald*, September 18, 1846, 2.

30. Resseguie, "A. T. Stewart's Marble Palace," 132. Resseguie notes that the term "Marble Palace" was first used in the *Herald*, September 18, 1846: "Stewart himself was in no way responsible for christening it with its unofficial title, and the term appears in neither his advertisements nor his letterhead." 150.

31. Resseguie notes that "at the end of the store's first week Bennett was still intrigued. Two of the *Herald*'s five front page columns were occupied to two thirds their length by two atrocious woodcuts—one representing the exterior of Stewart's new store and the other the interior of a competitor's (James M. Beck's) store" and that the articles were written by Bennett personally. Ibid., 145.

32. *New York Herald*, April 20, 1867, 6.

33. On the use of handbills in city streets, see David Henkin, *City Reading*.

34. Smith, *Sunshine and Shadow in New York*, 596.

35. Ibid., 596. When *Herald* reporters wanted to monopolize a commercial telegraph line to prevent other correspondents from reaching their papers, they were known to send lengthy passages of the Bible over the wire until the other newspaper's deadlines had passed. Ibid., 776.

36. Slight variations of the story of these transactions are recounted in Seitz, *The James Gordon Bennetts*, 150–52, and Carlson, *The Man Who Made News*, 378–80.

37. See Gardner, *The Architecture of Commercial Capitalism*.

38. Ibid., 151.

39. James D. McCabe wrote that the *Herald* building was "paved with marble tiles, and the desks, counters, racks, etc. are of solid black walnut, ornamented with plate glass. Everything is scrupulously clean, and the room presents the appearance

of some wealthy banking office." See McCabe, *Lights and Shadows of New York Life*, 248–49.

40. Gardner, *The Architecture of Commercial Capitalism*, 152.
41. Kennion, *The Architects' and Builders' Guide*, 49.
42. Ibid., 51.
43. See, for example, Hone, *The Diary of Philip Hone*.
44. See Le Bon, *The Crowd*.
45. See Gilje, *The Road to Mobocracy*, and Keller, *Triumph of Order.*
46. Quoted in Glaab and Brown, *The History of Urban America*, 55.
47. Wirth, "Urbanism as a Way of Life," 191.
48. McLuhan, *Understanding Media*, 349.
49. Wirth, "Urbanism," 192.
50. Park, et al. *The City*, 40.
51. Lindner, *The Reportage of Urban Culture*, 50.
52. Bridges, *Map of the City of New York*.
53. Spann, "The Greatest Grid," 14.
54. Ibid., 17.

CHAPTER 2. NEW BUILDINGS AND NEW SPACES

1. Here Greeley foreshadows the *Daily News*'s use of Abraham Lincoln's words on its building façade; the alignment with presidents represents an enduring and direct symbol of the relationship between the press and the state.
2. *New-York Tribune*, "City Items," April 12, 1841, 2.
3. Quoted in Baehr, *The New York Tribune Since the Civil War*, 7.
4. Greeley established the Tribune Association in 1849. He established one hundred shares of *Tribune* stock and split them between himself and his partner Thomas McElrath. From his own fifty shares Greeley offered employees the chance to buy as many as they could afford so they could share in the success in the newspaper. McElrath, however, held on to his shares, and it was not long before Greeley had only a minor interest in his own company. See Schulze, *Horace Greeley*, 24.
5. Hale, *Horace Greeley*, 303.
6. Clarke, *Frivolous Recollections*, 22. Biographers have noted that Dana was so embittered by the thought of being replaced at the *Tribune* that he took special aim at Reid's actions in his own newspaper, by referring to the *Tribune* as "Jay Gould's office."
7. The Whitelaw Reid Papers (hereafter WRP) are housed in the Library of Congress; a copy is housed in the Manuscripts and Archives Division of the New York Public Library.
8. WRP, January 23, 1873.
9. Ibid.
10. WRP, March 17, 1873.
11. Olmsted named several leading architects at Reid's request, including Cyrus Eidlitz who would later design the New York Times Building at Times Square, but he may have felt beholden to Hunt because Hunt's beautiful sculptures that had been commissioned for his Central Park design were never implemented.

12. Cortissoz, *The Life of Whitelaw Reid*, 301.

13. Ibid., 231.

14. *New-York Tribune*, April 10, 1875, 9.

15. Light and air were at a premium before the electric lighting was installed across the city. The Edison Electric Light Company provided some electric light to businesses in New York as early as 1878, but it was not until several years later that it was in all commercial structures. Thus tall towers with no immediate neighbors were highly prized for office space.

16. *New-York Tribune*, April 10, 1875, 9.

17. WRP, March 14, 1873.

18. See Bender and Taylor, "Culture and Architecture," 186.

19. *New-York Tribune*, "The Tribune's New Home," April 10, 1875.

20. Burnham, "Richard Morris Hunt Papers," 73.

21. *New-York Tribune*, "The New Tribune Building," June 7, 1873, 4.

22. Kluger, *The Paper*, 135.

23. *New-York Daily Times*, September 18, 1851, 1.

24. *New York Times*, May 26, 1858, 1.

25. M. Berger, *The Story of the New York Times*, 17.

26. *New York Times*, May 26, 1858, 1.

27. Davis, *History of the New York Times*, 47.

28. Turner, *When Giants Ruled*, 55–56.

29. *New York Times*, May 26, 1858, 1.

30. *Frank Leslie's Illustrated Newspaper* March 12, 1859, 225–26.

31. Ibid., 226.

32. M. Berger, *The Story of the New York Times*, 22.

33. Brown, *Raymond of the Times*.

34. Marshall, *Through America*, 12.

35. Davis, *History of the New York Times*, 165.

36. *New York Times*, "The New 'Times' Building," April 29, 1889, 4.

37. See, for example, *Scientific American, Architectural Record, Real Estate Record and Builders Guide*, and *American Architect and Building News*.

38. See Schuyler, "The Evolution of a Skyscraper," 329–43.

39. *New York Times*, Supplement, April 29 1889. The conscious use of the double-entendre words "stories" and "columns" when speaking of newspaper buildings seems not to have been realized, or at least articulated, until Adolf Loos's parodic submission for the Chicago Tribune Tower competition in 1922, which consisted of one gigantic Doric column. For a detailed account of this competition, see Katherine Solomonson's *The Chicago Tribune Tower Competition*.

40. Ironically, it was the construction of the Times Building that allowed Post to see the rust deterioration of the floor beams, which led him to conclude that the skyscraper form was dangerous and misguided. He continued, despite his own feelings, to build them for several more years, but registered his dissent in supporting laws that would restrict building heights. See Mausolf, *A Catalog of the Work of George B. Post*.

41. *Scientific American*, August 25 1888, 177.

42. King, *King's Handbook of New York City*, 618.

43. Allen Frank to George E. Jones, June 18, 1890, George E. Jones Papers, Box 1.

44. E. Prentiss Bailey to George E. Jones, George E. Jones Papers, Box 1.

45. Biggart, "Architectural Vignettes on Commercial Stationery," 24.

46. The final total of $1,114,467.37 is listed on page 41 of the 1888–1901 Job Book, in the George B. Post Collection.

47. Baker, *Richard Morris Hunt*, 222.

48. Davis, "The Journalism of New York," 226.

49. Elsaesser, "Early Film History and Multi-Media" 21.

50. *New York Times*, "Receiving the News," November 6, 1872, 8.

51. *New York Times*, "Waiting for the Returns Scenes in Front of the Newspaper Bulletin Boards," November 6, 1872, 8.

52. *New York Times*, "Proclaimed by the Times," November 8, 1893, 5.

53. *New York Times*, "New-York City Rejoices," November 9, 1892, 3.

54. *New York Sun*, "Human Sea Girts City Hall," November 9, 1904, 4.

55. *New York Times*, "News Promptly Given," November 6, 1895, 8.

56. Streible, "Children and the Mutoscope," 91–116.

57. *Chicago Daily Tribune*, "Prof. Elisha Gray Dead," January 22, 1901, 3.

58. *Knoxville Daily Journal*, April 12, 1868, 6.

59. *The Daily Inter Ocean*, "In the White City," September 23, 1893, 11.

60. *New York Sun*, November 7, 1906, 3.

61. *New-York Tribune*, November 3, 1909, 4.

62. *New York Sun*, November 7, 1906, 3.

## CHAPTER 3. NINETEENTH-CENTURY STORIES AND COLUMNS

1. Swanberg, *Pulitzer*, 95

2. Ibid.

3. Ibid., 74.

4. Ibid., 149.

5. Ibid. Swanberg also notes that Dana did not respond passively to this attempt at architectural bullying; he tried to thwart the building process by attempting to convince the city to use the land for a municipal courthouse.

6. *New York World*, April 11, 1888, 2.

7. Seitz, *Joseph Pulitzer*, 175.

8. *New York World*, December 10, 1890, Souvenir Supplement. As these were the two features most reviled by architectural critics, Post was likely relieved to relinquish responsibility for them to Pulitzer.

9. Ibid.

10. Ibid.

11. Ibid.

12. Ibid.

13. Ibid.

14. Ibid.

15. *Pictorial New York and Brooklyn*, 40.

16. *New York Times*, April 29, 1889, 10.

17. *New York World*, December 10, 1890, Souvenir Supplement.

18. Ibid. Due to ill health, Pulitzer himself was in treatment in Wiesbaden, Germany, at the time of the opening ceremony. His son was present in his place, and Pulitzer's famous "God grant . . ." address was cabled to the newspaper and read by someone else.

19. Churchill, *Park Row*, 43.

20. Swanberg, *Pulitzer*, 163.

21. O'Connor, *Scandalous Mr. Bennett*, 221.

22. Blumenfeld, *R.D.B.'s Diary*, 33.

23. *New York Times*, July 19, 1890, 8.

24. O'Connor, *Scandalous Mr. Bennett*, 222.

25. Bennett claimed that his life had been saved by an owl that woke him up after having drifted off while captaining a ship. As James Creelman remarked, "The bird that is awake and alert when all else is asleep is not a bad emblem for the *Herald*." Creelman, "The New York 'Herald' and its New Home," *Harper's Weekly*, 843.

26. Quoted in O'Connor, *Scandalous Mr. Bennett*, 224.

27. Creelman, "The New York 'Herald' and its New Home," 843.

28. O'Connor, *Scandalous Mr. Bennett*, 224.

29. Ibid.

30. Seitz, *The James Gordon Bennetts*, 360.

31. Hunt, "The Automatic Baseball Playograph," 195–98.

32. Shaw's Jewelry Shop across the street at 1341 Broadway brought nuisance charges against the *Herald* for business lost during these events and was awarded $729.59 in damages. See *Decisions of Supreme and Lower Courts of Record of New York State*, 655.

33. *New York Times*, August 22, 1903, 14.

34. *New York Times*, "Downtown Building Change," December 11, 1903, 2. These renovations are variously reported; van Leeuwen in 1903 (*Skyward Trend of Thought*, 111) and Landau and Condit in 1905 (*The Rise of the New York Skyscraper*, 297).

35. Sulzberger, *The New York Times*, 15.

36. *New York Times*, August 16, 1896, 1.

37. M. Berger, *The Story of the New York Times*, 113.

38. Ibid., 87–88.

39. Churchill, *Park Row*, 229.

40. *New York Times*, August 4, 1902, 1.

41. The subway station got this name as a result of its location in the basement of the Times Building; it immediately replaced the square's previous name.

42. Hearst could not secure rights to this land, and instead built his International Magazine Building (Joseph Urban and George B. Post & Sons, 1927–28) at 57th Street and 8th Avenue.

43. Landau and Condit, *The Rise of the New York Skyscraper*, 312.

44. *New York Times*, "Building Supplement," 7.

45. Ibid., 1.

46. Eco, "Function and Sign."

47. *New York Times,* "Building Supplement," 1.

48. Ibid., 5.

49. Ibid., 6.

50. Ibid., 8.

51. Ibid., 3.

52. Moss, *The American Metropolis,* 199.

53. Davis, *History of the New York Times,* 326.

54. Huxtable, "Re-inventing Times Square, " 356.

55. Dunlap, "Six Buildings that Share One Story," *New York Times,* November 14, 2001, 55.

CHAPTER 4. ART DECO NEWS

1. *New York Times,* April 10, 1921, 12.

2. Ogden Reid of the *New-York Tribune* bought the *Herald* from Frank Munsey, and announced that the combined paper would be published at the *Tribune*'s new home at 225 West 40th Street. "Reid Buys Herald from Munsey; Will Merge with Tribune," *New York Times,* March 18, 1924, 1.

3. Chapman, *Tell It to Sweeney,* 124.

4. Ibid., 134. See also *Printers Ink,* January 1923, 40–41.

5. Quoted in Chapman, *Tell It to Sweeney,* 142.

6. Alexander, "Vox Populi—I," 16.

7. *New York Daily News,* Publisher's Semi-Annual Statement, Audit Bureau of Circulations, September 30, 1920, 4.

8. McGivena, *The News,* 42.

9. Patterson Wire to Blossom, 1921, Joseph Medill Patterson Papers (hereafter JMPP) .

10. Joseph Medill Patterson (hereafter JMP) to William H. Field, July 8, 1919. JMPP, Box 15 Folder 1.

11. JMP to William H. Field, November 10, 1919. JMPP, Box 15 Folder 1.

12. JMP to Field, July 8, 1919. JMPP, Box 15, Folder 1.

13. JMP to Burke, August 23, 1921. JMPP, Box 16, Folder 3.

14. Editorial suggestions from Dick to Blossom, undated. JMPP, Box 15, Folder 3.

15. These circulation building "stunts" were not as well regarded by other papers. In Philadelphia, for example, then the country's third largest market, the *Bulletin* advertised that "Never has a single stunt been used to add circulation. Never a premium, prize, or contest. The Evening Bulletin reflects the sane, moderate spirit of a great people." *Philadelphia Bulletin* ad, *New Yorker,* May 26, 1928, 43.

16. Burke to JMP, April 18, 1921. JMPP, Box 16, Folder 4.

17. Swerling, "The Picture Papers Win," 455–58.

18. Merton E. Burke to JMP, 1920, and JMP Telegram to Field, July 14, 1920. JMPP, Box 16, Folder 1.

19. JMP to Field, August 19, 1919, JMPP, Box 15, Folder1.

20. McGivena, *The News,* 117.

21. Chapman, *Tell It to Sweeney*, 118.

22. "If the tenants persist in asking a ridiculous price, we recommend that you drop negotiations altogether and let it be known that you will proceed with your plans for demolition without affecting these particular premises. This will show these tenants that you do not need them and may result in their revising their ideas as to their holdup value." Letter from Chadbourne, Stanchfield & Levy to Hollis, July 28, 1928. JMPP, Box 15, Folder 9.

23. Chadbourne, Stanchfield & Levy to Hon. William E. Walsh, Chairman, Board of Standards and Appeals, November 20, 1928. JMPP, Box 15, Folder 9.

24. Hood had also designed radiator covers for the American Radiator Company prior to becoming that building's architect.

25. Solomonson, *The Chicago Tribune Tower Competition*, 6.

26. Horowitz and Sparkes, *The Towers of New York*, 2.

27. "Not Just a New Building—A New Standard" [ad], *New York Times*, February 21, 1930, 18.

28. Haskell, "The Stripes of the News," 713. Frank Lloyd Wright, among others, has taken credit for convincing Hood to lop off whatever was on top in early designs.

29. Fenske, *The Skyscraper and the City*, 25.

30. Haskell, "The Stripes of the News," 713.

31. "Just after the Daily News Building was finished with its straight, white-bricked lines, an acquaintance tapped him on the shoulder at a party. 'Don't say a word! I know just what you had in mind when you did the News job. You were piling newspapers, hot from the press, in great white piles. Clever. Very Clever.'" Hood agreed. His own codicil to the story is "All I had in mind was four and half foot windows every nine feet." Talmey, "Man Against The Sky."

32. Hood, *Architectural Forum*.

33. Kilham, *Raymond Hood*, 19.

34. Marchand, *Advertising the American Dream*, 279.

35. JMP to Arthur Clarke, May 5, 1919, JMPP, Box 16, Folder 6.

36. "Manhattan's Building Peak Shifts to Forty-second Street," *New York Times*, February 3, 1929.

37. "Glamour," [ad] *New York Times*, July 9, 1929, 21.

38. Barr, "Preface," 14.

39. "The Lobby of the News Building: 220 East 42nd Street, New York," promotional pamphlet. JMPP, Box 15, Folder 9.

40. Kilham, *Raymond Hood*, 25.

41. In advertising for tenants for the new building, the publicity manager for the News Syndicate Company, Leo McGivena, revealed a prejudice for the most efficient advertising media: "It is suggested that the expenditure be restricted to two New York morning papers in addition to the *News*—The *Times* and the *Herald Tribune*. While the *Sun* and the *Post* undoubtedly have considerable merit as real estate media, nevertheless they must duplicate to a great extent these two morning papers." The campaign was also to run in the *Chicago Tribune*, but no other publications or

magazines were included. Leo McGivena, "News Building Advertising" memo to Douglas Elliman Company, January 28, 1929, JMPP, Box 15, Folder 9.

42. McGivena, *The News*, 185.

43. Alexander, "Vox Populi—II," 25.

44. "Glamour," [ad] *New York Times*, July 9, 1929, 21

45. Chapman, *Tell It to Sweeney*, 118.

46. See JMPP, Box 12 for correspondence with RCA, NAB, and others.

47. Griswold, "Nine Years Ago," 145.

48. Haskell, "The Stripes of the News," 713.

49. Woolf, "An Architect Hails the Rule of Reason."

50. North, *Raymond Hood*, 11.

51. Biggart, "Architectural Stationery in Commercial Printing," 31.

52. It is also not entirely clear who was responsible for the decision to build the 45th Street structure, as Hearst had recently sold the *Daily Mirror* to Alexander J. Kobler, although many suspected that Hearst himself was still in charge.

53. "The New Home of the New York Tribune" [ad], *New-York Tribune*, April 28, 1922, 11; April 17, 1923.

54. Editorial, *New-York Tribune*, April 15, 1923.

55. The building was completed by the engineering firm Lockwood, Green & Co., a Boston practice known principally for its factories, including the Acme Wire Company in New Haven and the Seth Thomas Clock Company in Thomaston, Connecticut; the Diamond Match Company in Oshkosh, Wisconsin; and the Shef-field Car Company in Three Rivers, Michigan. The same firm would soon build the Wall Street Journal plant at 33rd Street and Tenth Avenue, and the press structure at the *Daily News*, as well as the conversion of 220 South Street from the *Journal American* to the *New York Post*. Dolke, "Some Essentials in the Construction of an Industrial Building."

56. See Martin, *The Organizational Complex*.

57. "The Tribune to Move Up Town Into a Big, New Model Plant," *New-York Tribune*, December 16, 1921, 1.

58. Editorial, *New-York Tribune*, April 15, 1923.

59. *The New York Evening Post Founded by Alexander Hamilton*, 44–45; Nevins, *The Evening Post*.

60. That Park Row had ceased to be the center of news production was made clear in Schiff's note to her managing editor, "Where's Park Row?"

CHAPTER 5. POSTWAR NEWS

1. *PM*, "Paper Deliverers Vote 1648 to 41 to Strike," July 1, 1945.

2. *Chicago Tribune*, "Strike Jobless in North East Near 100,000," June 28, 1945, 27.

3. Kluger, *The Paper*, 397.

4. *PM*, July 3, 1945.

5. *PM*, July 2, 1945, 10.

6. Berelson, "What 'Missing the Newspaper' Means."

7. Mullen, "N.Y. Newspaper Strike Puts Reader on Cash-Carry Basis," 1.

8. "Hear the Harvard-Yale Game by Radio at the Tribune Building," *New-York Tribune*, November 24, 1922.

9. *PM*, "With Mirrors," July 2, 1945.

10. *PM*, "City Queues" July 9, 1945, 10.

11. "Newspaper Strike," *New York Times*, July 8, 1945, 27.

12. *Seventeen Days*, Daily News, 1945.

13. *PM*, "Paper Deliverers," July 1, 1945.

14. Milkman, *PM: A New Deal in Journalism*, 40.

15. Ibid., 48–56.

16. Ibid., 73.

17. *New York Times*, "PM to Print in Own Plant," May 27, 1944, 13.

18. *PM*, July 2, 1945.

19. Lewis, Editorial, *PM*, July 2, 1945.

20. "Ailing Big-City Dailies," *Wall Street Journal*, December 20, 1962, 32.

21. Ibid.

22. "Whaddya Read?" *Wall Street Journal*, December 11, 1962, 32.

23. Robert F. Bryan to John Hay Whitney, August 1, 1957. Quoted in Kluger, *The Paper*, 528–29.

24. Kluger, *The Paper*, 581.

25. Ibid., 655.; Wise, "The Crisis in Newspaper Row," 110–13.

26. "Text of Statement on Papers' Merger," *New York Times*, March 22, 1966, 28; "Three New York Newspapers Set Merger Ending One Afternoon, One Sunday Issue," *Wall Street Journal*, March 22, 1966, 4.

27. Phillips, "A Paper's Death Evokes Silence, Then Banter," 14.

28. Schiff, "Dear Reader."

29. Quoted in Nissenson, *The Lady Upstairs*, 255.

30. "Journal Building is Bought by Post," *New York Times*, September 17, 1967, 33.

31. "Post to Introduce Printing in Four Colors," *New York Times*, April 16, 1968, 95.

32. Paul Sann to Dorothy Schiff, April 8, 1971. Dorothy Schiff Papers, Box 155, Folder 7.

33. Greenberg, *Branding New York*, 100.

34. Lankevich, *New York City*, 210.

35. *Daily News*, October 30, 1975.

36. Greenberg, *Branding New York*, 237.

37. *New York Times*, June 20, 1965.

EPILOGUE

1. Lyons, "Central Park Jazzed for AOL/TW Home."

2. Ibid.

3. Furman, "Shareholders in Revolt," 39.

4. "McFarlane Buys Stake in AOL Time Warner Building," *New York Sun*, February 4, 2003, 9.

5. Vise, "Time Warner Sheds 'AOL' From Its Name."

6. Finnigan, "AOL Time Warner Reboots Building Plans," 12.

7. Rose, "Keyword: Context."

8. Hearst Building, Landmarks Preservation Commission Report, 1987.

9. Nash and McGrath, *Manhattan Skyscrapers*, 45.

10. Ibid.

11. Editorial letter, Hearst Newspapers, May 29, 1927.

12. Winkler, "Notes on an American Phenomenon," 22.

13. Pogrebin, "Norman Foster's Hearst Tower Makes its Mark on Manhattan," 1.

14. Noland, "Hearst Tower—Re-inventing the Skyscraper."

15. See Light and Wallace, "Not Out of the Woods," 3–20.

16. "Hearst Tower" brochure, 2.

17. Ibid., 4.

18. The building received a Gold Rating from the Leadership in Energy and Environmental Design rating system, and was awarded an Energy Star designation in 2010.

19. Rice, "Glass Steel Whiz Chosen to Design New Hearst Tower," 6.

20. Goldberger, "Dream House," 110                    .

21. Goldberger, "Spiffing up the Gray Lady," 21.

22. Glancy, "The Power of the Tower," 23.

23. Ibid.

24. Muschamp, "A Rare Opportunity for Real Architecture Where it's Needed," B1.

25. Ibid.

26. "Thousands Watch Times Bulletins," *New York Times*, November 7, 1928, 17.

27. "Huge Times Sign Will Flash News," *New York Times*, November 8, 1928, 30.

28. Berman, "A Times Square for the New Millennium."

29. Sassen, *Cities in a World Economy*, 66.

30. Taylor, "Broadway," 228.

31. Berger, "Near Newspaper Row of Years Gone by, the Media Return," A21; Sederstrom, "Lower Manhattan Gains Ground as Publishing Hub," B6.

# Bibliography

"Ailing Big-City Dailies," *Wall Street Journal*, December 20, 1962.

Alexander, Jack. "Vox Populi—I," *New Yorker*, August 6, 1938, 16.

———. "Vox Populi—II," *New Yorker*, August 13, 1938, 25.

Baehr, Harry W. Jr. *The New York Tribune Since the Civil War*. New York: Dodd, Mead & Co., 1936.

Baker, Paul R. *Richard Morris Hunt*. Cambridge: MIT Press, 1980.

Barr, Alfred H. Jr. "Preface." In *The International Style: Architecture Since 1922*, by Henry-Russell Hitchcock Jr. and Philip Johnson. New York: W.W. Norton & Co., 1932.

Barth, Gunther. *City People: The Rise of Modern City Culture in Nineteenth-Century America*. New York and London: Oxford University Press, 1980.

Bender, Thomas and William R. Taylor. "Culture and Architecture: Some Aesthetic Tensions in the Shaping of Modern New York City." In *Visions of the Modern City: Essays in History, Art, and Literature*, ed. William Sharpe and Leonard Wallock. Baltimore: Johns Hopkins University Press, 1987.

Bennett, James Gordon. *New York Herald*, September 18, 1846, 2.

Berelson, Bernard. "What 'Missing the Newspaper' Means," in *Communication Research 1948–49*, ed. P. F. Lazarsfeld and F. N. Stanton. New York: Harper & Brothers, 1949.

Berger, Joseph. "Near Newspaper Row of Years Gone by, the Media Return," *New York Times*, January 29, 2011, A21.

Berger, Meyer. *The Story of the New York Times, 1851–1951*. New York: Times, Inc., 1951.

Berman, Marshall. "A Times Square for the New Millennium: Life on the Cleaned up Boulevard," *Dissent Magazine*, Winter 2006.

Bessie, Simon Michael. *Jazz Journalism: The Story of the Tabloid Newspaper*. New York: E.P. Dutton & Co. Inc., 1938.

Biggart, Robert. "Architectural Stationery in Commercial Printing." *Ephemera* 8 (1995).

Blumenfeld, Ralph. *R.D.B.'s Diary 1887–1914*. London: W. Heinemann, Ltd., 1930.

Bridges, William. *Map of the City of New York and Island of Manhattan with Explanatory Remarks and References*. New York: William Bridges, 1811.

Brown, Francis. *Raymond of the Times*. New York: W.W. Norton, 1951.

Browne, Junius Henri. *The Great Metropolis: A Mirror of New York*. Hartford: American Publishing Co., 1869.

Burnham, Alan Ed. "Richard Morris Hunt Papers." Unpublished manuscript. American Architectural Archives.

Carey, James. "Technology and Ideology: The Case of the Telegraph." In *Prospects: An Annual of American Cultural Studies*, ed. Jack Salzman. Cambridge: Cambridge University Press, 1983.

Carlson, Oliver. *The Man Who Made News: James Gordon Bennett.* New York: Duell, Sloan and Pearce, 1942.

Chapman, John. *Tell It to Sweeney: The Informal History of the New York Daily News.* Garden City, NY: Doubleday, 1961.

Churchill, Allen. *Park Row.* New York: Rinehart, 1958.

"City Items," *New-York Tribune*, April 12, 1841, 2.

"City Queues," *PM*, July 9, 1945, 10.

Clarke, Selah F. *Frivolous Recollections of the Humble Side of Old Days in New York Newspaperdom.* New York: American Press, 1932.

Comstock, W. T. *Architecture and Building* 63 (1961).

Cortissoz, Royal. *The Life of Whitelaw Reid.* New York: C. Scribner's Sons, 1921.

Creelman, James. "The New York 'Herald' and its New Home," *Harper's Weekly*, September 2, 1893.

Crouthamel, James. *Bennett's New York Herald and the Rise of the Popular Press.* Syracuse: Syracuse University Press, 1989.

Davis, Elmer. *History of the New York Times, 1851–1921.* New York: New York Times Co., 1921.

Davis, Hartley. The Journalism of New York." *Munsey's Magazine* (November 1900): 217–33.

*Decisions of Supreme and Lower Courts of Record of New York State.* New York Supplement 156. St. Paul, MN: West Publishing Company, 1916.

Dolke, Fred W. Jr. "Some Essentials in the Construction of an Industrial Building." *American Architect* 111, no. 2148 (February 1917).

Dorothy Schiff Papers, 1904–1989, Manuscripts and Archives Division, New York Public Library.

"Downtown Building Change," *New York Times*, December 11, 1903, 2.

Dunlap, David. "Six Buildings that Share One Story," *New York Times*, November 14, 2001, 55.

Eco, Umberto. "Function and Sign: The Semiotics of Architecture," In *Signs, Symbols and Architecture*, ed. G. Broadbent, R. Bunt, and C. Jencks. New York: John Wiley & Sons, 1980.

Editorial letter, Hearst Newspapers, May 29, 1927. In *Selections from the Writings and Speeches of William Randolph Hearst.* San Francisco: 1948, 443.

Editorial, *New-York Tribune*, April 15, 1923.

Elsaesser, Thomas. "Early Film History and Multi-Media: An Archaeology of Possible Futures?" In *New Media, Old Media: A History and Theory Reader*, ed. Wendy Hui Kyong Chun and Thomas Keenan. New York: Taylor & Francis, 2006.

Fenske, Gail. *The Skyscraper and the City: The Woolworth Building and the Making of Modern New York.* Chicago: University of Chicago Press, 2008.

Finnigan, David. "AOL Time Warner Reboots Building Plans," *Brandweek*, June 24, 2002.

*Frank Leslie's Illustrated Newspaper,* March 12, 1859.

Furman, Phyllis. "Shareholders in Revolt," *Daily News,* May 17, 2002, 39.

Gardner, Deborah. *The Architecture of Commercial Capitalism: John Kellum and the Development of New York, 1840–1875.* Ph.D. Thesis. Columbia University, 1979.

Gilje, Paul A. *The Road to Mobocracy: Popular Disorder in New York City, 1763–1834.* Chapel Hill: University of North Carolina Press, 1987.

Glaab, Charles N., and Theodore Brown. *The History of Urban America.* New York: MacMillan Company, 1967.

"Glamour" [ad], *New York Times,* July 9, 1929, 21.

Glancy, Jonathan. "The Power of the Tower," *Guardian* (Manchester, England), November 26, 2007, 23.

Goldberger, Paul. "Dream House," *New Yorker,* October 30, 2000, 110.

———. "Spiffing up the Gray Lady," *New Yorker,* January 7, 2002, 21.

Greenberg, Miriam. *Branding New York: How a City in Crisis Was Sold to the World.* New York and London: Routledge, 2008.

Griswold, J. B. "Nine Years Ago Raymond M. Hood Was Behind in His Rent, Today He Holds the Spotlight As a Master Showman of Steel and Stone," *American Magazine* (1931): 145.

Hale, William Harlan. *Horace Greeley: Voice of the People.* Collier, 1961.

Haskell, Douglas. "The Stripes of the News," *The Nation,* December 24, 1930.

Hearst Building, Landmarks Preservation Commission Report, 1987.

"Hearst Tower," brochure.

"Hear the Harvard-Yale Game by Radio at the Tribune Building," *New-York Tribune,* November 24, 1922.

Henkin, David. *City Reading: Written Words and Public Spaces in Antebellum New York.* New York: Columbia University Press, 1998.

Hobsbawm, Eric. *The Invention of Tradition.* Cambridge University Press, 1983.

Hone, Philip. *The Diary of Philip Hone,* ed. Bayard Tuckerman, 2 vols. New York: Dodd, Mead, 1889.

Hood, Raymond. *Architectural Forum,* 1930.

Horowitz, Louis, and Boyden Sparkes. *The Towers of New York: The Memoirs of a Master Builder.* New York: Simon and Schuster, 1937.

"Huge Times Sign Will Flash News," *New York Times,* November 8, 1928, 30.

"Human Sea Girts City Hall," *New York Sun,* November 9, 1904, 4.

Hunt, J. "The Automatic Baseball Playograph," *Yale Scientific Monthly* 19 (December 1912): 195–98.

Huxtable, Ada Louise. "Re-inventing Times Square, 1900." In Taylor, *Inventing Times Square.*

"In the White City," *The Daily Inter Ocean,* September 23, 1893, 11.

Jackson, Kenneth T. *The Great Metropolis: Poverty and Progress in New York City.* New York: American Heritage, 1993.

Jones, George E. Papers, 1811–91. New York Public Library, Manuscripts and Archives Division.

"Journal Building is Bought by Post," *New York Times,* September 17, 1967, 33.

Keller, Lisa. *Triumph of Order: Democracy and Public Space in New York and London.* New York: Columbia University Press, 2009.

Kennion, John. *The Architects' and Builders' Guide.* New York: Fitzpatrick & Hunter, 1868.

Kilham, Walter H. Jr. *Raymond Hood, Architect: Form through Function in the American Skyscraper.* New York: Architectural Publishing Co., 1973.

King, Moses. *King's Handbook of New York City,* 2nd ed. Boston: Moses King, 1892.

Kluger, Richard. *The Paper: The Life and Death of the New York Herald Tribune.* New York: Knopf, 1986.

*Knoxville Daily Journal,* April 12, 1868, 6.

Lancaster, Paul. *Gentleman of the Press: The Life and Times of an Early Reporter, Julian Ralph, of the Sun.* Syracuse: Syracuse University Press, 1992.

Landau, Sarah, and Carl Condit. *The Rise of the New York Skyscraper, 1865–1913.* New Haven, CT: Yale University Press, 1999.

Lankevich, George. *New York City: A Short History.* New York: New York University Press, 2002.

Le Bon, Gustave. *The Crowd: A Study of the Popular Mind.* New York: Viking, 1960.

Lewis, John P. Editorial, *PM,* July 2, 1945.

Light, Andrew, and Aurora Wallace. "Not Out of the Woods: Preserving the Human in Environmental Architecture," *Environmental Values* 14 (2005): 3–20.

Lindner, Rolf. *The Reportage of Urban Culture: Robert Park and the Chicago School.* Cambridge: Cambridge University Press, 2006.

Lippman, Walter. *Public Opinion.* New York: Harcourt Brace and Company, 1922.

Lyons, Charles. "Central Park Jazzed for AOL/TW Home," *Variety,* May 30, 2002.

"Manhattan's Building Peak Shifts to Forty-Second Street," *New York Times,* February 3, 1929.

Marchand, Roland. *Advertising the American Dream: Making Way for Modernity, 1920–1940.* Berkeley: University of California Press, 1985.

———. *Creating the Corporate Soul: The Rise of Public Relations and Corporate Imagery in American Big Business.* Berkeley: University of California Press, 2001.

Marquis, James. *The Metropolitan Life.* New York: Arno Press, 1947.

Marshall, Walter Gore. *Through America: or, Nine Months in the United States.* London: Sampson Low, Marston, Searle & Rivington, 1881.

Martin, Reinhold. *The Organizational Complex: Architecture, Media, and Corporate Space.* Cambridge: MIT Press, 2003.

Mausolf, Lisa. *A Catalog of the Work of George B. Post, Architect.* M.S. Thesis, Columbia University, 1983.

McCabe, James D. *Lights and Shadows of New York Life, or, The Sights and Sensations of the Great City.* National Publishing, 1872. New York: Farrar, Straus and Giroux, 1970.

"McFarlane Buys Stake in AOL Time Warner Building *New York Sun,*" February 4, 2003, 9.

McGivena, Leo. *The News: The First Fifty Years of New York's Picture Newspaper.* New York: New York News Syndicate Co, 1969.

McGurl, Mark. "Making It Big: Picturing the Radio Age in *King Kong,*" *Critical Inquiry* 22, no. 3 (Spring 1996).

McLuhan, Marshall. *Understanding Media: The Extensions of Man.* New American Library, 1964.

Milkman, Paul. *PM: A New Deal in Journalism, 1940–1948.* New Brunswick, NJ: Rutgers University Press, 1997.

Moss, Frank. *The American Metropolis, from Knickerbocker Days to the Present Time: New York City Life in All its Various Phases.* 3 vols. New York: P.F. Collier, 1897.

Mullen, Robert R. "N.Y. Newspaper Strike Puts Reader on Cash-Carry Basis," *Christian Science Monitor,* July 2, 1945, 1.

Muschamp, Herbert. "A Rare Opportunity for Real Architecture Where It's Needed," *New York Times,* October 22, 2000, B1.

Nash, Eric, and Norman McGrath. *Manhattan Skyscrapers.* New York: Princeton Architectural Press, 2010.

Nevins, Allan. *The Evening Post: A Century of Journalism.* New York: Boni and Liveright, 1922.

"The New Home of the New York Tribune" [ad], *New-York Tribune.* April 28, 1922, 11; April 17, 1923.

"Newspaper Strike," *New York Times,* July 8, 1945, 27.

"News Promptly Given," *New York Times,* November 6, 1895, 8.

"The New 'Times' Building," *Daily Times,* April 29, 1889.

"The New Tribune Building," *New-York Tribune,* June 7, 1873.

"New-York City Rejoices," *New York Times,* November 9, 1892, 3.

*New York Daily News.* Publisher's Semi-Annual Statement, Audit Bureau of Circulations, September 30, 1920, 4.

*The New York Evening Post Founded by Alexander Hamilton 1801–1925.* New York: New York Evening Post, 1925.

*New York Times.* "Building Supplement," April 29 1889, 7.

*New York World.* Souvenir Supplement, December 10, 1890.

Nissenson, Marilyn. *The Lady Upstairs: Dorothy Schiff and the New York Post.* New York: St. Martins Press, 2007.

Noland, David. "Hearst Tower—Re-inventing the Skyscraper," *Popular Mechanics,* April 1, 2006.

North, Arthur Tappan. *Raymond Hood.* New York and London: McGraw-Hill Book Company, 1931.

"Not Just a New Building—A New Standard" [ad], *New York Times,* February 21, 1930, 18.

O'Brien, Frank M. *The Story of the Sun: New York, 1833–1918.* New York: George H. Doran Co., 1918.

O'Connor, Richard. *The Scandalous Mr. Bennett.* New York: Doubleday, 1962.

"The Old and New Tribune Buildings," *New-York Tribune,* May 17, 1873, 6.

"Paper Deliverers Vote 1648 to 41 to Strike," *PM,* July 1, 1945.

Park, Robert E., E. W. Burgess, Roderick Duncan McKenzie, and Louis Wirth. *The City.* Chicago: University of Chicago Press, 1925.

Patterson, Joseph Medill. Papers [JMPP]. Lake Forest University Archives, Lake Forest, IL.

Phillips, McCandlish. "A Paper's Death Evokes Silence, Then Banter," *New York Times*, May 6, 1967.

*Pictorial New York and Brooklyn: a Guide to the Same, and Vicinity*. New York: Smith, Bleakley & Co., 1892.

"PM to Print in Own Plant," *New York Times*, May 27, 1944, 13.

Pogrebin, Robin. "Norman Foster's Hearst Tower Makes its Mark on Manhattan," *New York Times*, June 6, 2006, 1.

Post, George B. Collection. Print and Architecture Library, New York Historical Society.

"Post to Introduce Printing in Four Colors," *New York Times*, April 16, 1968, 95.

Pray, Isaac Clark. *Memoirs of James Gordon Bennett and His Times*. New York: Stringer and Townsend, 1855.

"Proclaimed by the Times," *New York Times*, November 8, 1893, 5.

"Prof. Elisha Gray Dead," *Chicago Daily Tribune*, January 22, 1901, 3.

"Receiving the News," *New York Times*, November 6, 1872.

"Reid Buys Herald from Munsey; Will Merge with Tribune," *New York Times*, March 18, 1924, 1.

Reid, Whitelaw. Papers [WRP]. Library of Congress, Washington, DC.

Resseguie, Harry E. "A. T. Stewart's Marble Palace—The Cradle of the Department Store," *New York Historical Society Quarterly* (April 1964): 132.

Rice, Andrew. "Glass Steel Whiz Chosen to Design New Hearst Tower," *New York Observer*, February 26, 2001, 6.

Rose, Frank. "Keyword: Context," *Wired*, December 1996.

Sassen, Saskia. *Cities in a World Economy*. Thousand Oaks, CA: Pine Forge Press, 1994.

Schiff, Dorothy. "Dear Reader," *New York Post*, December 27, 1953.

Schudson, Michael. *Discovering the News: A Social History of American Newspapers*. New York: Basic Books, 1978.

Schulze, Suzanne. *Horace Greeley: A Bio-Bibliography*. New York: Greenwood Press, 1992.

Schuyler, Montgomery. "The Evolution of a Skyscraper," *Architectural Record*, November 14, 1903.

Sederstrom, Jotham. "Lower Manhattan Gains Ground as Publishing Hub," *New York Times*, November 24, 2010, B6.

Seitz, Don. *The James Gordon Bennetts, Father and Son, Proprietors of the New York Herald*. Indianapolis: Bobbs-Merrill, 1928.

———. *Joseph Pulitzer: His Life and Letters*. New York: Simon and Schuster, 1924.

*Seventeen Days: A Story of Newspaper History in the Making*. Daily News, 1945.

Shachtman, Tom. *Skyscraper Dreams: The Great Real Estate Dynasties of New York*. New York: iUniverse, 2001.

Smith, Matthew Hale. *Sunshine and Shadow in New York*. Hartford: J.B. Burr Publishing Co., 1883.

Solomonson, Katherine. *The Chicago Tribune Tower Competition: Skyscraper Design and Cultural Change in the 1920s*. Cambridge: Cambridge University Press, 2001.

Spann, Edward K. "The Greatest Grid: The New York Plan of 1811." In *Two Centuries of American Planning*, ed. Daniel Schaffer. London: Mansell Publishing Ltd., 1988.

Steele, Janet. *The Sun Shines for All: Journalism and Ideology in the Life of Charles A. Dana.* Syracuse: Syracuse University Press, 1993.

Stone, Candace. *Dana and "The Sun."* New York: Dodd Mead & Company, 1938.

Streible, Dan. "Children and the Mutoscope," *Cinémas* 14, no. 1 (Fall 2003): 91–116.

"Strike Jobless in North East Near 100,000," *Chicago Tribune,* June 28, 1945, 27.

Sulzberger, Arthur H. *The New York Times, 1851–1951: A Centenary Address.* New York and San Francisco: Newcomen Society in North America, 1951.

Swanberg, W. A. *Pulitzer.* New York: Charles Scribner's Sons, 1967.

Swerling, Jo. "The Picture Papers Win," *The Nation,* October 21, 1925: 455–58.

Talmey, Allene. "Man Against The Sky," *New Yorker,* April 11, 1931: 27.

Taylor, William R. "Broadway: The Place That Words Built." In Taylor, *Reinventing Times Square.*

———. "The Evolution of Public Space in New York City: The Commercial Showcase of America." In *Consuming Visions: Accumulation and Display of Goods in America, 1880–1920,* ed. Simon J. Bronner. New York and London: W.W. Norton & Company, 1989.

———. *Reinventing Times Square.* Baltimore: John Hopkins University Press, 1996.

"Text of Statement on Papers' Merger," *New York Times,* March 22, 1966.

"Thousands Watch Times Bulletins," *New York Times,* November 7, 1928, 17.

"Three New York Newspapers Set Merger Ending One Afternoon, One Sunday Issue," *Wall Street Journal,* March 22, 1966, 4.

"Towers of Babel," *New York Times,* March 7, 1920, 2.

"The Tribune's New Home," *New-York Tribune,* April 10, 1875.

"The Tribune to Move Up Town into a Big, New Model Plant," *New-York Tribune,* December 16, 1921.

Turner, Hy B. *When Giants Ruled: The Story of Park Row, New York's Great Newspaper Street.* New York: Fordham University Press, 1999.

Van Leeuwen, Thomas A. *Skyward Trend of Thought: The Metaphysics of the American Skyscraper.* Cambridge: MIT Press, 1990.

Vise, David A. "Time Warner Sheds 'AOL' from Its Name," *Washington Post,* October 17, 2003, E1.

"Waiting for the Returns Scenes in Front of the Newspaper Bulletin Boards," *New York Times,* November 6, 1872, 8.

Warner, Michael. *The Letters of the Republic: Publication and the Public Sphere in Eighteenth-Century America.* Cambridge: Harvard University Press, 1990.

"Whaddya Read?" *Wall Street Journal,* December 11, 1962, 32.

Winkler, John. "Notes on an American Phenomenon," *New Yorker,* May 21, 1927, 22.

Wirth, Louis. "Urbanism as a Way of Life," *American Journal of Sociology* 44, no. 1 (July 1938).

Wise, T. A. "The Crisis in Newspaper Row," *Fortune,* October 1964, 110–13.

"With Mirrors," *PM,* July 2, 1945.

Woolf, S. J. "An Architect Hails the Rule of Reason," *New York Times Magazine,* November 1, 1931.

# Index

AURORA WALLACE is a professor in the department of Media, Culture, and Communication at New York University and the author of *Newspapers and the Making of Modern America*.

# The History of Communication

The University of Illinois Press
is a founding member of the
Association of American University Presses.

---

Composed in 10/13.5 Janson Text LT Std
with Electra LT Std display
by Barbara Evans
at the University of Illinois Press
Manufactured by Thomson-Shore, Inc.

University of Illinois Press
1325 South Oak Street
Champaign, IL 61820-6903
www.press.uillinois.edu